Mat[

Practice in the Basic Skills

C000142804

Contents

Addition

A

4 + 7 = ☐	7 + 3 = ☐	8 + 3 = ☐	9 + 8 = ☐	5 + 7 = ☐
3 + 8 = ☐	8 + 5 = ☐	9 + 2 = ☐	4 + 6 = ☐	7 + 4 = ☐
9 + 4 = ☐	9 + 3 = ☐	5 + 6 = ☐	5 + 8 = ☐	8 + 8 = ☐
5 + 5 = ☐	7 + 9 = ☐	8 + 6 = ☐	7 + 7 = ☐	3 + 9 = ☐
3 + 7 = ☐	9 + 5 = ☐	9 + 1 = ☐	4 + 8 = ☐	9 + 6 = ☐
8 + 4 = ☐	6 + 6 = ☐	7 + 8 = ☐	4 + 9 = ☐	6 + 4 = ☐
6 + 9 = ☐	7 + 5 = ☐	6 + 5 = ☐	9 + 7 = ☐	8 + 9 = ☐
6 + 7 = ☐	6 + 8 = ☐	9 + 9 = ☐	2 + 8 = ☐	2 + 9 = ☐
5 + 9 = ☐	7 + 6 = ☐	8 + 7 = ☐	1 + 9 = ☐	7 + 2 = ☐

B

36	58	29	87	42
+29	+61	+76	+46	+75

82	26	69	27	98
+19	+54	+49	+86	+94

C

27 + 53 + 47 = ☐ 　　　　　　　89 + 32 + 20 = ☐

78 + 16 + 8 = ☐ 　　　　　　　39 + 29 + 45 = ☐

28 + 82 + 16 = ☐ 　　　　　　　54 + 6 + 29 = ☐

44 + 29 + 82 = ☐ 　　　　　　　29 + 81 + 14 = ☐

7 + 81 + 32 = ☐ 　　　　　　　88 + 22 + 53 = ☐

D

303	421	606	82	524
+76	+199	+98	+119	+309

499	408	600	390	702
+277	+192	+477	+29	+193

E

1 Two hundred and ninety-six plus fifty-five.
2 Find the sum of 279, 609 and 87.
3 What is two hundred and two more than sixty-nine?
4 Add together fifty-six, eighty-nine and one hundred.
5 What is the total of 347, 629, 45 and 102?

Addition

A

19 + 1 = ☐	78 + 7 = ☐	17 + 7 = ☐	36 + 7 = ☐	14 + 9 = ☐
48 + 3 = ☐	39 + 6 = ☐	75 + 5 = ☐	53 + 8 = ☐	26 + 8 = ☐
29 + 2 = ☐	28 + 6 = ☐	91 + 9 = ☐	38 + 4 = ☐	63 + 9 = ☐
47 + 4 = ☐	85 + 9 = ☐	24 + 8 = ☐	86 + 5 = ☐	79 + 3 = ☐
36 + 7 = ☐	81 + 9 = ☐	69 + 4 = ☐	37 + 3 = ☐	58 + 5 = ☐
89 + 5 = ☐	96 + 6 = ☐	34 + 7 = ☐	72 + 8 = ☐	88 + 9 = ☐
43 + 7 = ☐	94 + 6 = ☐	55 + 8 = ☐	76 + 4 = ☐	45 + 7 = ☐
27 + 8 = ☐	59 + 7 = ☐	65 + 6 = ☐	18 + 2 = ☐	97 + 9 = ☐
99 + 9 = ☐	67 + 6 = ☐	49 + 8 = ☐	68 + 8 = ☐	57 + 5 = ☐

B

267	404	1369	2009	4521
+2300	+692	+7609	+5999	+2209

4206	3092	432	989	6293
+96	+274	+8492	+9009	+2938

C

46 + 2204 + 3008 = ☐   6204 + 439 + 2009 = ☐

126 + 729 + 2929 = ☐   7420 + 207 + 893 = ☐

674 + 2067 + 7246 = ☐   924 + 6231 + 1625 = ☐

2004 + 3247 + 2584 = ☐   8909 + 99 + 387 = ☐

6125 + 1008 + 922 = ☐   1547 + 4272 + 804 = ☐

D
1. Increase two thousand and sixty-six by four hundred and eighty-nine.
2. Find the sum of 2791, 4726, 909 and 12.
3. Ninety-nine plus two hundred and seventy-six plus five thousand, three hundred and fifty-nine.
4. What number is seven hundred and sixty-two more than three thousand, five hundred and forty-nine?
5. Add 4541, 2679, 3452 and 19.

Subtraction

A

18 – 9 = ☐	11 – 2 = ☐	14 – 6 = ☐	13 – 8 = ☐	10 – 4 = ☐
11 – 6 = ☐	15 – 7 = ☐	10 – 9 = ☐	12 – 4 = ☐	16 – 7 = ☐
12 – 7 = ☐	11 – 4 = ☐	14 – 7 = ☐	10 – 6 = ☐	12 – 6 = ☐
11 – 8 = ☐	10 – 2 = ☐	13 – 9 = ☐	12 – 3 = ☐	17 – 9 = ☐
10 – 7 = ☐	13 – 4 = ☐	12 – 5 = ☐	10 – 8 = ☐	14 – 5 = ☐
16 – 9 = ☐	11 – 3 = ☐	10 – 5 = ☐	12 – 9 = ☐	13 – 6 = ☐
13 – 7 = ☐	17 – 8 = ☐	11 – 7 = ☐	10 – 3 = ☐	15 – 9 = ☐
11 – 9 = ☐	10 – 1 = ☐	14 – 8 = ☐	11 – 5 = ☐	15 – 8 = ☐
12 – 8 = ☐	15 – 6 = ☐	13 – 5 = ☐	14 – 9 = ☐	16 – 8 = ☐

B

427	204	830	472	634
−76	−194	−509	−98	−328

525	400	632	520	906
−329	−307	−76	−417	−509

C Find the difference between the following numbers.

276 and 429   862 and 599

306 and 900   172 and 645

841 and 469   1000 and 799

29 and 547   627 and 433

209 and 604   42 and 293

D Find the missing numbers.

☐05	46☐	7☐3	420	7☐0
−3☐9	− 27	−☐21	−☐ 7	−629
176	4☐6	552	63	1☐1

74☐	☐91	4☐7	8☐0	54☐
−☐31	−296	−8☐	−113	−434
209	29☐	341	☐87	1☐6

Subtraction

A

28 – 9 = ☐	47 – 8 = ☐	33 – 7 = ☐	74 – 6 = ☐	60 – 5 = ☐
42 – 4 = ☐	23 – 7 = ☐	71 – 8 = ☐	44 – 8 = ☐	81 – 7 = ☐
21 – 5 = ☐	41 – 3 = ☐	50 – 6 = ☐	76 – 7 = ☐	72 – 9 = ☐
100 – 1 = ☐	90 – 2 = ☐	63 – 4 = ☐	91 – 6 = ☐	53 – 5 = ☐
64 – 7 = ☐	44 – 9 = ☐	92 – 7 = ☐	70 – 4 = ☐	30 – 9 = ☐
95 – 8 = ☐	35 – 6 = ☐	84 – 5 = ☐	43 – 6 = ☐	82 – 8 = ☐
32 – 5 = ☐	61 – 9 = ☐	66 – 8 = ☐	31 – 4 = ☐	56 – 9 = ☐
51 – 2 = ☐	80 – 3 = ☐	25 – 7 = ☐	85 – 9 = ☐	82 – 8 = ☐
40 – 7 = ☐	37 – 9 = ☐	52 – 3 = ☐	20 – 8 = ☐	93 – 9 = ☐

B

1047 –926	6302 –3027	4007 –2416	5200 –4927	3472 –989
8280 –5397	3047 –2076	5552 –3479	1007 –939	2160 –1234

C Find the difference between the following numbers.

5072 and 1699	8411 and 939
727 and 3271	4327 and 6745
9231 and 5421	3271 and 9909
687 and 5343	726 and 6003
4110 and 7216	8414 and 3333

D

8012 minus 4716	1009 subtract 821
2009 minus 1921	4717 subtract 2090
8721 minus 923	5423 subtract 737
9414 minus 2099	2040 subtract 1629
3204 minus 1474	9998 subtract 8999

E
1 How much is 4796 greater than 3726?
2 How much is 3002 less than 6001?
3 Decrease 4296 by 2741.
4 Decrease 7179 by 4298.

Multiplication

A

2 × 2 = ☐	7 × 3 = ☐	12 × 5 = ☐	9 × 4 = ☐	9 × 6 = ☐
6 × 3 = ☐	10 × 2 = ☐	8 × 6 = ☐	6 × 5 = ☐	5 × 2 = ☐
8 × 5 = ☐	0 × 5 = ☐	4 × 2 = ☐	3 × 2 = ☐	12 × 3 = ☐
11 × 6 = ☐	6 × 6 = ☐	5 × 3 = ☐	11 × 3 = ☐	5 × 5 = ☐
9 × 2 = ☐	11 × 4 = ☐	8 × 4 = ☐	6 × 2 = ☐	7 × 4 = ☐
12 × 4 = ☐	0 × 6 = ☐	10 × 5 = ☐	6 × 4 = ☐	3 × 3 = ☐
8 × 2 = ☐	10 × 3 = ☐	0 × 4 = ☐	7 × 5 = ☐	7 × 2 = ☐
12 × 6 = ☐	12 × 2 = ☐	11 × 2 = ☐	10 × 6 = ☐	4 × 4 = ☐
9 × 5 = ☐	5 × 4 = ☐	9 × 3 = ☐	0 × 3 = ☐	0 × 2 = ☐
8 × 3 = ☐	11 × 5 = ☐	7 × 6 = ☐	10 × 4 = ☐	4 × 3 = ☐

B

347	1271	2010	879	1532
×6	×5	×4	×2	×3

1249	2347	1416	799	876
×3	×2	×5	×4	×6

C

1007 × 6	927 × 5	2071 × 4
3412 × 2	876 × 6	3099 × 3
509 × 6	1247 × 3	1672 × 6
2144 × 4	2438 × 2	1764 × 5

D Find the product of the following numbers.

2073 and 4	1743 and 5
869 and 6	4023 and 2

E **1** What number is four times six hundred and seventy-five?

2 Find the total of 176 + 176 + 176 + 176 + 176 by multiplication.

Multiplication

A

0 × 7 = ☐	11 × 9 = ☐	2 × 9 = ☐	8 × 7 = ☐	3 × 8 = ☐
6 × 8 = ☐	10 × 8 = ☐	3 × 7 = ☐	0 × 11 = ☐	10 × 12 = ☐
12 × 9 = ☐	7 × 7 = ☐	12 × 12 = ☐	4 × 9 = ☐	0 × 9 = ☐
11 × 11 = ☐	6 × 12 = ☐	5 × 9 = ☐	5 × 8 = ☐	12 × 8 = ☐
3 × 12 = ☐	4 × 11 = ☐	8 × 8 = ☐	9 × 7 = ☐	11 × 7 = ☐
4 × 8 = ☐	6 × 9 = ☐	2 × 7 = ☐	10 × 9 = ☐	9 × 8 = ☐
12 × 7 = ☐	5 × 7 = ☐	12 × 11 = ☐	2 × 11 = ☐	0 × 8 = ☐
9 × 9 = ☐	2 × 9 = ☐	4 × 12 = ☐	5 × 12 = ☐	6 × 11 = ☐
5 × 11 = ☐	0 × 12 = ☐	3 × 9 = ☐	11 × 8 = ☐	10 × 7 = ☐
2 × 8 = ☐	10 × 11 = ☐	6 × 7 = ☐	4 × 7 = ☐	3 × 11 = ☐

B

2171	4326	1749	4007	2106
×7	×12	×9	×8	×11

6050	3741	5020	3205	1989
×11	×9	×12	×8	×7

C

2146 × 8	4161 × 12	943 × 9
5100 × 7	5240 × 11	1245 × 12
2471 × 9	1009 × 7	2035 × 8
3062 × 11	7214 × 8	6021 × 7

D Multiply:

4271 by 8	2161 by 9	4029 by 11
3029 by 7	936 by 12	3274 by 9

E

1 Find the product of two thousand four hundred and sixty-two and seven.

2 What number is nine times as big as four thousand six hundred and twenty-four?

Division

A

54 ÷ 6 = ☐	36 ÷ 4 = ☐	60 ÷ 5 = ☐	21 ÷ 3 = ☐	4 ÷ 2 = ☐
18 ÷ 3 = ☐	20 ÷ 2 = ☐	30 ÷ 5 = ☐	10 ÷ 2 = ☐	48 ÷ 6 = ☐
6 ÷ 2 = ☐	36 ÷ 3 = ☐	0 ÷ 5 = ☐	40 ÷ 5 = ☐	8 ÷ 2 = ☐
36 ÷ 6 = ☐	33 ÷ 3 = ☐	15 ÷ 3 = ☐	25 ÷ 5 = ☐	66 ÷ 6 = ☐
44 ÷ 4 = ☐	12 ÷ 2 = ☐	28 ÷ 7 = ☐	32 ÷ 4 = ☐	18 ÷ 2 = ☐
50 ÷ 5 = ☐	24 ÷ 6 = ☐	9 ÷ 3 = ☐	48 ÷ 4 = ☐	0 ÷ 6 = ☐
14 ÷ 2 = ☐	35 ÷ 5 = ☐	30 ÷ 3 = ☐	16 ÷ 2 = ☐	0 ÷ 4 = ☐
24 ÷ 2 = ☐	60 ÷ 6 = ☐	22 ÷ 2 = ☐	16 ÷ 4 = ☐	72 ÷ 6 = ☐
27 ÷ 3 = ☐	20 ÷ 4 = ☐	0 ÷ 3 = ☐	45 ÷ 5 = ☐	0 ÷ 2 = ☐
42 ÷ 6 = ☐	12 ÷ 3 = ☐	40 ÷ 4 = ☐	55 ÷ 5 = ☐	24 ÷ 2 = ☐

B

2)252	3)715	5)605	6)618	4)814
6)870	3)348	2)947	5)271	4)823

C

6)5454	2)1632	5)2002	6)1461	3)2234
5)3604	2)1419	6)3726	3)1212	5)2753

D

1. What is a quarter of 4260?
2. Divide 1470 by 3.
3. How many must be added to 4369 to make it divide exactly by 6?
4. Two hundred and seventy children travel on 5 coaches. How many on each coach?
5. How many groups of four are there in six thousand five hundred and twenty?
6. Share 8005 between 5.
7. By how much is one sixth of 9102 greater than one third of 3948?

Division

A

24 ÷ 8 = ☐	56 ÷ 7 = ☐	18 ÷ 2 = ☐	99 ÷ 9 = ☐	0 ÷ 7 = ☐
21 ÷ 7 = ☐	0 ÷ 11 = ☐	120 ÷ 12 = ☐	80 ÷ 8 = ☐	48 ÷ 8 = ☐
49 ÷ 7 = ☐	144 ÷ 12 = ☐	0 ÷ 9 = ☐	36 ÷ 9 = ☐	108 ÷ 9 = ☐
72 ÷ 12 = ☐	121 ÷ 11 = ☐	40 ÷ 8 = ☐	45 ÷ 9 = ☐	96 ÷ 8 = ☐
64 ÷ 8 = ☐	63 ÷ 7 = ☐	44 ÷ 11 = ☐	36 ÷ 12 = ☐	77 ÷ 7 = ☐
90 ÷ 9 = ☐	72 ÷ 8 = ☐	14 ÷ 2 = ☐	32 ÷ 8 = ☐	54 ÷ 9 = ☐
84 ÷ 12 = ☐	132 ÷ 11 = ☐	0 ÷ 8 = ☐	22 ÷ 11 = ☐	35 ÷ 7 = ☐
48 ÷ 12 = ☐	18 ÷ 9 = ☐	66 ÷ 11 = ☐	60 ÷ 12 = ☐	81 ÷ 9 = ☐
88 ÷ 8 = ☐	27 ÷ 9 = ☐	70 ÷ 7 = ☐	0 ÷ 12 = ☐	55 ÷ 11 = ☐
42 ÷ 7 = ☐	33 ÷ 11 = ☐	16 ÷ 8 = ☐	110 ÷ 11 = ☐	28 ÷ 7 = ☐

B

7)945	8)992	9)965	11)937	8)640
12)758	7)910	9)918	12)708	11)849

C

7)1450	12)4836	11)5727	8)7452	9)4726
11)3289	12)4236	8)3203	7)4378	9)3250

D Find the missing numbers.

$$\begin{array}{r} 4\ ☐\ 6 \\ 7\overline{)2\ 9\ 8\ 2} \end{array} \qquad \begin{array}{r} ☐\ 9\ 5 \\ 9\overline{)3\ 5\ 5\ 5} \end{array} \qquad \begin{array}{r} 5\ ☐\ 6 \\ 8\overline{)4\ 0\ 4\ 8} \end{array} \qquad \begin{array}{r} 5\ 2\ ☐ \\ 12\overline{)6\ 3\ 4\ 8} \end{array} \qquad \begin{array}{r} 2\ ☐\ 5 \\ 12\overline{)2\ 9\ 4\ 0} \end{array}$$

$$\begin{array}{r} 6\ 0\ 7 \\ 11\overline{)6\ 6\ ☐\ 7} \end{array} \qquad \begin{array}{r} 2\ 0\ 2 \\ 7\overline{)1\ ☐\ 1\ 4} \end{array} \qquad \begin{array}{r} 3\ 3\ 0 \\ 8\overline{)☐\ 6\ 4\ 0} \end{array} \qquad \begin{array}{r} 1\ 8\ 1 \\ 11\overline{)☐\ 9\ 9\ 1} \end{array} \qquad \begin{array}{r} 8\ 1\ 8 \\ 8\overline{)6\ 5\ 4\ ☐} \end{array}$$

E

4371 ÷ 7	6271 ÷ 9	7143 ÷ 8	4321 ÷ 12
6002 ÷ 11	5050 ÷ 8	6242 ÷ 9	7000 ÷ 12

F Share:

2240 by 7	3488 by 8	3491 by 11
6480 by 12	4761 by 9	4249 by 7

Averages

A Find the average of each line of numbers.

29	23	25	27		
82	98	107	132	144	151
60	43	56	72	19	
26	34	51	25	16	19	25

B The heights of 5 boys were 124 cm, 138 cm, 162 cm, 150 cm, 141 cm.

1 What was the average height?

2 How many boys were above the average height?

3 How many boys were below the average height?

4 What was the difference between the height of each boy and the average height?

C

name	test 1	test 2	test 3	test 4
Anni	19	15	20	15
Jade	18	14	19	16
Maya	17	17	18	17
Freya	16	12	19	17
Jess	15	12	19	15
av. mark				

1 What was the average mark in each test?

2 Who was above average in 3 tests?

3 Who was below average in 3 tests?

4 Who scored the average in 3 tests?

D

name	weight
Connor	34 kg
Jack	35 kg
Rob	38 kg
Alfie	39 kg
Henry	40 kg
Zack	43 kg
Dev	46 kg
Paul	45 kg

1 What is the total weight of the boys?

2 What is the average weight of the boys?

3 How many boys are above the average weight?

4 How many boys are below the average weight?

5 Which boy has the average weight?

6 If Connor, Jack, Rob and Alfie each gained 2 kg in weight, what would the average now be?

7 If the total weight became 360 kg, what would the new average be?

8 If Henry was absent what would the average be?

Long multiplication

A **1** Write in words the value of the underlined figure in each of these numbers.

32<u>4</u>6	5<u>2</u>17	62<u>9</u>0	<u>3</u>299	745<u>6</u>	<u>8</u>291
621<u>5</u>	6<u>8</u>14	<u>5</u>023	32<u>6</u>1	4<u>4</u>21	50<u>5</u>2
53<u>7</u>1	<u>3</u>291	141<u>6</u>	72<u>9</u>1	3<u>8</u>24	<u>5</u>678

2 Multiply each number by 10 and then write the new value of each underlined figure.

B

36	47	54	70	82	59
×10	×10	×10	×10	×10	×10

45	63	79	92	25	18
×20	×20	×20	×20	×20	×20

39	81	37	62	75	43
×30	×30	×30	×30	×30	×30

53	47	29	69	54	73
×40	×40	×40	×40	×40	×40

C

21	52	63	19	84	76
×50	×90	×50	×90	×80	×60

92	48	37	18	29	54
×60	×70	×50	×80	×70	×90

Long multiplication

A

27	41	59	82	74
×16	×14	×13	×17	×15

86	93	74	69	19
×17	×18	×16	×19	×13

B

17	86	54	72	65
×31	×91	×21	×81	×41

33	62	48	28	94
×21	×51	×71	×41	×61

C

86	37	24	53	67
×27	×59	×43	×64	×72

16	43	73	99	85
×94	×81	×52	×36	×77

D

147	236	419	262	531
×20	×70	×40	×60	×50

674	801	345	354	720
×80	×90	×30	×30	×50

E

525	906	372	741	506
×96	×45	×37	×83	×64

471	261	633	152	819
×59	×23	×74	×78	×35

Long division

A

21⟌63   21⟌42   31⟌62   41⟌82   21⟌84   31⟌93

19⟌38   19⟌95   29⟌87   19⟌57   29⟌58   19⟌76

B

21⟌76   31⟌74   21⟌89   31⟌99   21⟌47   41⟌87

19⟌63   19⟌52   19⟌99   19⟌46   29⟌92   19⟌81

C

21⟌147   21⟌189   21⟌126   21⟌105   21⟌168

19⟌171   19⟌133   29⟌174   19⟌152   19⟌114

D

21⟌175   21⟌137   21⟌125   21⟌200   21⟌156

19⟌179   19⟌164   19⟌147   19⟌131   19⟌159

E

18⟌90   13⟌52   15⟌75   13⟌78   16⟌80

17⟌68   17⟌85   14⟌56   14⟌84   15⟌90

F

15⟌50   16⟌69   18⟌79   13⟌63   17⟌80

14⟌85   18⟌77   16⟌39   16⟌98   15⟌98

G

24⟌168   13⟌104   14⟌126   27⟌135   17⟌153

23⟌161   15⟌135   28⟌168   18⟌108   16⟌112

H

27⟌169   17⟌146   26⟌139   24⟌200   18⟌165

Long division

A

19)228   21)231   19)209   31)341   19)266

29)377   21)273   39)468   21)252   31)372

B

31)961   19)988   41)902   21)672   39)897

19)722   21)903   19)893   29)667   21)441

C

19)776   21)645   29)589   39)412   19)578

31)642   21)851   19)392   21)440   41)449

D

16)514   13)683   17)724   23)773   15)946

27)852   18)974   24)770   14)593   28)598

E

19)1374   14)1162   39)1192   15)1365   24)1988

16)1403   29)2053   27)1701   49)2113   18)1566

F

16)3424   17)5651   22)9927   19)7904   21)6741

18)7399   13)7957   14)4074   15)2586   23)4899

G

27)5535   13)2993   26)2756   23)4616   14)4760

15)6045   16)9613   17)8536   24)9840   21)6300

H

41)1743   13)4721   27)989   23)4721   29)7071

19)647   39)1192   18)4050   15)7642   17)6986

Problems – Long multiplication and division

1   A plot of ground has 23 rows of lettuce with 16 in each row. How many lettuce altogether?

2   How many groups of 16 are there in 336?

3   There are 21 classes in a school and 525 rulers to be shared among them.
    a   How many rulers per class?   **b**   How many rulers left over?

4   A T.V. costing £75·60 is paid for in 24 instalments. How much is each instalment?

5   A shelf holds 134 cartons of soap. How many cartons will 25 shelves hold?

6   A coach holds 44 children. How many coaches are needed to carry
    a   375 children   **b**   528 children   **c**   594 children?

7   A box holds 144 packets of sweets. How many packets will be held by
    a   36 boxes   **b**   28 boxes   **c**   45 boxes?

8   Five hundred and four bottles of milk were delivered to a school. Each class had 39 bottles. If there were 12 classes, how many bottles were left over?

9   £994 is shared equally among 14 people. How much does each person receive?

10   A matchbox holds 48 matches. How many matches in 135 boxes?

11   A piece of cloth measuring 15 metres cost £48·60. Find the cost of
    a   1 metre   **b**   13 m   **c**   25 m

12   What is the product of five hundred and thirty-nine, and fifty-four?

Money notation

A   Write these amounts of money in words.

£4·72   £3·06   69p   £24·22   £41·00   45p

B   Complete:

1   214p = £   406p = £   259p = £

606p = £   472p = £   205p = £

302p = £   167p = £   321p = £

2   £3·24 =   p   £5·21 =   p   £11·05 =   p

£6·18 =   p   £4·17 =   p   £5·17 =   p

£19·04 =   p   £0·23 =   p   £0·73 =   p

3   £1·25 = £   +   tens +   ones

£2·72 = £   +   tens +   ones

£5·04 = £   +   tens +   ones

£7·12 = £   +   tens +   ones

£4·18 = £   +   tens +   ones

C   What is the value of the figure underlined in each of these amounts of money?

£4·2<u>7</u>   £<u>1</u>1·16   £21·<u>4</u>0   £<u>2</u>04·70   £6·3<u>2</u>

£2<u>1</u>4·75   £<u>2</u>7·62   £1<u>2</u>·54   £<u>6</u>21·43   £0·<u>7</u>2

D   Write out these amounts of money in order of size with the largest first.

1	55p	550p	£5·05	£5·55	£0·54	£55·00
2	11p	£1·10	£115	115p	£0·15	£0·01
3	£3·00	303p	34p	£0·35	£3·02	£0·03
4	606p	£6·60	66p	£0·65	£0·06	£6·66
5	£2·12	£2·03	213p	23p	£0·22	£2·02

Money notation

A

	£1	50p	20p	10p	5p	2p	1p
A	1	1	4	5	6	3	2
B	2		5	4	3	2	1
C	5	5	1	3	4	1	
D	6	3	2	1	7	9	5
E	2	6	7	3	6	12	1
F		8	1	5	9	4	7

A,B,C,D,E,F, are moneyboxes.

1   How much does each contain?

2   What is the total amount of money?

B   Give the value of these bags of coins in £ notation.

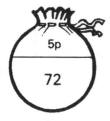
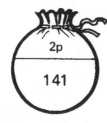

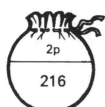
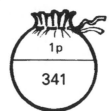
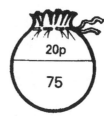
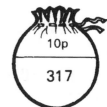

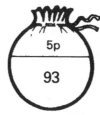
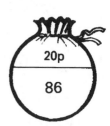

C   Write down the notes and coins needed to make up these amounts of money using the fewest possible.

£0·37   £4·26   £7·18   £0·78   £11·06

£7·22   £5·73   £2·14   £22·96   £12·86

D   Write how many   **a** 1p   **b** 2p   **c** 5p   **d** 10p   coins are needed to make each of these amounts.

£1·50   £3·40   £9·70   £4·30   £8·10

Money – addition and subtraction

A

$£4·17 + £2·24 + £0·25 =$

$£3·06 + £10·73 + £8·40 =$

$£12·17 + £19·21 + £0·76 =$

$£0·82 + £14·35 + £11·16 =$

$£11·13 + £0·47 + £0·73 =$

$£4·62 + £7·26 + £24·30 =$

$£12·04 + £1·75 + £16·25 =$

$£40·19 + £14·12 + £0·88 =$

$£36·76 + £29·14 + £0·63 =$

$£5·24 + £4·21 + £4·32 =$

$£19·45 + £12·72 + £16·43 =$

$£24·16 + £32·45 + £17·92 =$

$£0·39 + £0·16 + £34·10 =$

$£17·22 + £22·11 + £17·41 =$

$£45·16 + £35·16 + £12·81 =$

$£0·82 + £45·29 + £0·87 =$

$£3·35 + £7·13 + £2·06 =$

$£4·24 + £12·42 + £0·47 =$

$£12·52 + £15·89 + £0·98 =$

$£19·18 + £6·47 + £1·35 =$

B

$£12·62 − £9·81 =$

$£19·47 − £15·82 =$

$£24·98 − £21·69 =$

$£15·27 − £12·45 =$

$£35·18 − £26·17 =$

$£41·17 − £32·86 =$

$£12·14 − £9·47 =$

$£19·76 − £12·68 =$

$£21·24 − £19·35 =$

$£35·32 − £34·76 =$

$£16·24 − £7·21 =$

$£19·29 − £18·24 =$

$£32·17 − £29·54 =$

$£46·19 − £32·27 =$

$£28·45 − £0·49 =$

$£52·17 − £33·18 =$

$£24·12 − £19·45 =$

$£18·47 − £7·67 =$

$£33·45 − £29·85 =$

$£29·16 − £17·40 =$

C

$£42·36 + £29·27 − £35·26 =$

$£21·21 + £42·73 − £45·37 =$

Money – multiplication and division

A

£4·17	£10·16	£24·13	£16·70
×4	×5	×8	×7

£0·96	£12·26	£24·27	£29·17
×8	×3	×8	×4

£12·17	£32·15	£28·36	£41·12
×9	×5	×4	×2

£16·04	£16·29	£0·99	£32·72
×12	×6	×5	×2

£22·75	£15·55	£27·43	£10·71
×3	×7	×8	×9

B

$6\overline{)£6·84}$	$12\overline{)£27·84}$	$2\overline{)£14·74}$	$11\overline{)£42·13}$
$9\overline{)£28·26}$	$3\overline{)£12·06}$	$10\overline{)£45·70}$	$5\overline{)£0·65}$
$2\overline{)£63·24}$	$12\overline{)£47·16}$	$8\overline{)£48·32}$	$5\overline{)£24·40}$
$7\overline{)£33·04}$	$4\overline{)£10·96}$	$6\overline{)£134·52}$	$8\overline{)£173·84}$
$9\overline{)£10·80}$	$3\overline{)£54·81}$	$4\overline{)£141·76}$	$7\overline{)£113·26}$

C What is

$\frac{1}{6}$ of £12·72? $\frac{1}{4}$ of £5·04? $\frac{1}{3}$ of £8·13?

$\frac{1}{9}$ of £15·57? $\frac{1}{7}$ of £24·36? $\frac{1}{8}$ of £32·40?

Money problems

1. What is the total of £4·72 + £8·73 + £9·27?

2. By how much is £27·16 greater than £24·05?

3. Find the cost of 5 rackets at £4·95 each.

4. A worker received £43·50 for 6 hours work. How much per hour was he paid?

5. A shopkeeper bought a toy for £2·75. He sold it for £3·60. What was his profit?

6. If eggs are sold at 10p each, how much would 24 eggs cost?

7. A hotel bill was £117·30 for 3 days. What was the cost per day?

8. How much would be saved by paying £22·86 for a watch instead of buying it with 8 payments of £3·04?

9. How much change did John receive from a £10·00 note after he had spent £6·47?

10. What is the total cost of 5 ices at 20p each, and 7 soft drinks at 25p each?

11. John spent £4·25 and Jane £3·95 at the bookshop. **a** How much did they spend altogether? **b** How much more did John spend?

12. Six boys shared the cost of a train set costing £47·04. How much did each boy pay?

Bills

Find the total cost of each of these bills.

1 4 oranges at 9p each   =

$1\frac{1}{2}$ kg of potatoes
at 36p a kg   =

$\frac{1}{2}$ kg of tomatoes at
74p a kg   =

$\frac{1}{2}$ kg of apples at
56p a kg   =_____
                        total

2 $1\frac{1}{2}$ kg of margarine at
48p a kg   =

2 dozen eggs at
6p each   =

$\frac{1}{2}$ kg of potatoes at
36p a kg   =

5 litres of milk at
60p a litre   =_____
                        total

3 4 jars of jam at
49p a jar   =

6 jellies at 21p each   =

2 jars of mincemeat
at 54p a jar   =

3 packets of rice at
46p a packet   =_____
                        total

4 4 pairs of socks at
£1·83 a pair   =

3 shirts at £15·79 each   =

6 handkerchiefs at
42p each   =

3 ties at £6·50 each   =

1 pair of pyjamas at
£8·25   =_____
                        total

5 6 ices at 19p each   =

5 drinks at 63p each   =

7 bags of crisps at
55p each   =

6 fruit sundaes at
37p each   =_____
                        total

6 2 kg of sugar at
59p a kg   =

200 g of pressed
meat at 42p per 100 g   =

$1\frac{1}{2}$ kg of margarine at
48p a kg   =

4 tins of coffee at
97p a tin   =_____
                        total

Fractions

What fraction of each of these shapes is: **a** shaded?   **b** unshaded?

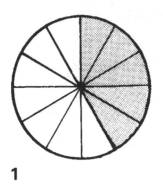

1

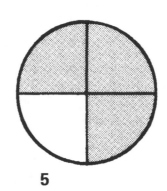

2

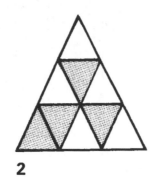

3

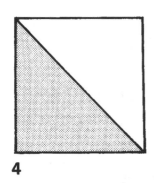

4

5

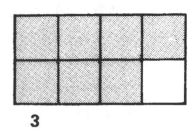

6

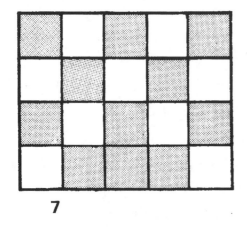

7

8

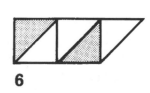

9

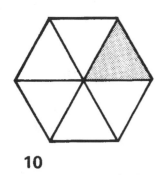

10

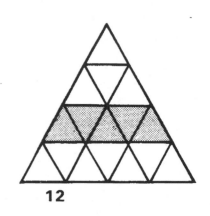

11

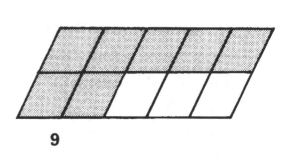

12

Fractions

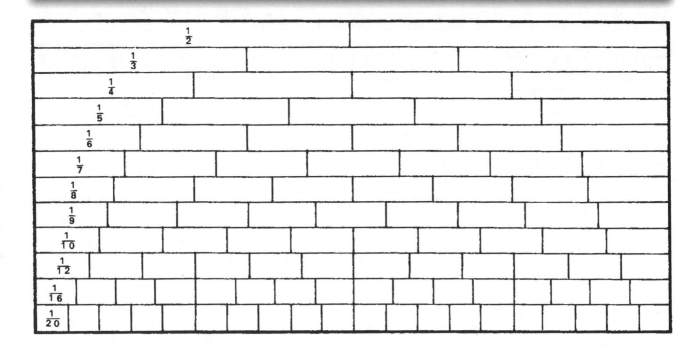

Use the chart to make equivalent fractions.

$\frac{9}{10} = \frac{}{20}$ $\qquad$ $\frac{4}{5} = \frac{}{10}$ $\qquad$ $\frac{1}{3} = \frac{}{9}$ $\qquad$ $\frac{4}{6} = \frac{}{12}$

$\frac{2}{3} = \frac{4}{}$ $\qquad$ $\frac{16}{20} = \frac{8}{}$ $\qquad$ $\frac{3}{4} = \frac{15}{}$ $\qquad$ $\frac{3}{8} = \frac{6}{}$

$\frac{1}{4} = \frac{}{8}$ $\qquad$ $\frac{1}{2} = \frac{}{10}$ $\qquad$ $\frac{4}{10} = \frac{2}{}$ $\qquad$ $\frac{7}{8} = \frac{14}{}$

$\frac{}{5} = \frac{6}{10}$ $\qquad$ $\frac{8}{12} = \frac{}{3}$ $\qquad$ $\frac{}{20} = \frac{1}{10}$ $\qquad$ $\frac{6}{12} = \frac{1}{}$

$\frac{}{20} = \frac{3}{10}$ $\qquad$ $\frac{5}{} = \frac{10}{16}$ $\qquad$ $\frac{8}{20} = \frac{}{10}$ $\qquad$ $\frac{12}{} = \frac{3}{4}$

$\frac{}{20} = \frac{7}{10}$ $\qquad$ $\frac{5}{6} = \frac{10}{}$ $\qquad$ $\frac{8}{} = \frac{1}{2}$ $\qquad$ $\frac{2}{6} = \frac{}{3}$

$\frac{4}{} = \frac{1}{2}$ $\qquad$ $\frac{5}{20} = \frac{1}{}$ $\qquad$ $\frac{1}{6} = \frac{}{12}$ $\qquad$ $\frac{2}{} = \frac{6}{9}$

$\frac{4}{20} = \frac{1}{}$ $\qquad$ $\frac{6}{8} = \frac{}{4}$ $\qquad$ $\frac{4}{} = \frac{1}{4}$ $\qquad$ $\frac{}{20} = \frac{3}{5}$

$\frac{10}{20} = \frac{1}{}$ $\qquad$ $\frac{2}{} = \frac{1}{5}$ $\qquad$ $\frac{2}{4} = \frac{}{6}$ $\qquad$ $\frac{8}{} = \frac{16}{20}$

$\frac{6}{8} = \frac{}{20}$ $\qquad$ $\frac{}{9} = \frac{4}{12}$ $\qquad$ $\frac{4}{16} = \frac{}{20}$ $\qquad$ $\frac{5}{} = \frac{2}{8}$

Fractions

A   What denominator is needed for these fractions?

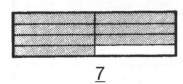   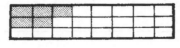   

$\underline{7}$ $\underline{5}$ $\underline{7}$

B $\frac{3}{5} = \frac{6}{10}$ $\frac{1}{2} = \frac{5}{10}$ so $\frac{3}{5} > \frac{1}{2}$

Find a common denominator for each of these pairs of fractions and then put in > or < or =.

$\frac{4}{5}$ $\frac{7}{10}$ $\frac{5}{6}$ $\frac{2}{3}$ $\frac{15}{20}$ $\frac{3}{4}$ $\frac{9}{12}$ $\frac{4}{6}$ $\frac{13}{20}$ $\frac{7}{10}$

$\frac{3}{4}$ $\frac{5}{6}$ $\frac{2}{3}$ $\frac{3}{4}$ $\frac{1}{2}$ $\frac{2}{5}$ $\frac{3}{4}$ $\frac{5}{8}$ $\frac{17}{20}$ $\frac{4}{5}$

C $\frac{8}{16} = \frac{1}{2}$ The fraction is now in its lowest terms.

Rewrite these fractions in lowest terms.

$\frac{16}{20}$ $\frac{5}{15}$ $\frac{12}{16}$ $\frac{12}{18}$ $\frac{9}{12}$ $\frac{20}{40}$ $\frac{6}{8}$ $\frac{14}{20}$ $\frac{8}{10}$ $\frac{25}{30}$

D   Rewrite these mixed numbers as improper fractions.

$3\frac{1}{2}$ $7\frac{1}{4}$ $1\frac{3}{5}$ $4\frac{2}{3}$ $6\frac{1}{10}$ $2\frac{3}{8}$ $3\frac{5}{6}$ $1\frac{3}{20}$ $2\frac{2}{15}$ $3\frac{5}{9}$

E   Rewrite these improper fractions as mixed numbers.

$\frac{15}{4}$ $\frac{13}{10}$ $\frac{21}{8}$ $\frac{17}{6}$ $\frac{23}{20}$ $\frac{13}{2}$ $\frac{29}{5}$ $\frac{35}{6}$ $\frac{19}{12}$ $\frac{22}{9}$

F   Rewrite as mixed numbers in lowest terms.

$\frac{16}{10}$ $\frac{36}{8}$ $\frac{45}{10}$ $\frac{24}{20}$ $\frac{16}{12}$ $\frac{25}{15}$ $\frac{18}{4}$ $\frac{20}{14}$ $\frac{28}{24}$ $\frac{32}{6}$

Addition of fractions

Leave your answers in simplest form.

A $\frac{3}{5} + \frac{1}{5} =$ $\frac{3}{10} + \frac{5}{10} =$ $\frac{7}{20} + \frac{9}{20} =$ $\frac{5}{12} + \frac{5}{12} =$

     $\frac{3}{16} + \frac{5}{16} =$ $\frac{3}{8} + \frac{3}{8} =$ $\frac{7}{15} + \frac{7}{15} =$ $\frac{1}{6} + \frac{3}{6} =$

B $\frac{3}{5} + \frac{3}{5} =$ $\frac{7}{8} + \frac{5}{8} =$ $\frac{7}{12} + \frac{11}{12} =$ $\frac{5}{6} + \frac{5}{6} =$

     $\frac{17}{20} + \frac{11}{20} =$ $\frac{7}{10} + \frac{9}{10} =$ $\frac{11}{16} + \frac{15}{16} =$ $\frac{6}{7} + \frac{6}{7} =$

C $\frac{2}{5} + \frac{3}{10} =$ $\frac{1}{2} + \frac{1}{4} =$ $\frac{1}{4} + \frac{5}{8} =$ $\frac{7}{20} + \frac{3}{5} =$

     $\frac{7}{16} + \frac{3}{8} =$ $\frac{1}{6} + \frac{7}{12} =$ $\frac{17}{20} + \frac{1}{40} =$ $\frac{1}{3} + \frac{4}{9} =$

D $\frac{4}{5} + \frac{7}{10} =$ $\frac{3}{4} + \frac{5}{12} =$ $\frac{9}{20} + \frac{3}{5} =$ $\frac{5}{6} + \frac{11}{12} =$

     $\frac{6}{7} + \frac{11}{14} =$ $\frac{4}{5} + \frac{7}{15} =$ $\frac{19}{24} + \frac{7}{12} =$ $\frac{7}{8} + \frac{3}{4} =$

E $\frac{1}{6} + \frac{3}{8} =$ $\frac{2}{3} + \frac{1}{4} =$ $\frac{1}{2} + \frac{2}{5} =$ $\frac{5}{6} + \frac{1}{9} =$

     $\frac{1}{2} + \frac{2}{9} =$ $\frac{5}{12} + \frac{3}{8} =$ $\frac{1}{3} + \frac{3}{8} =$ $\frac{3}{5} + \frac{1}{4} =$

F $\frac{2}{3} + \frac{7}{8} =$ $\frac{7}{9} + \frac{1}{2} =$ $\frac{9}{10} + \frac{1}{4} =$ $\frac{11}{12} + \frac{3}{8} =$

     $\frac{7}{8} + \frac{5}{6} =$ $\frac{7}{12} + \frac{5}{8} =$ $\frac{19}{25} + \frac{7}{10} =$ $\frac{8}{9} + \frac{5}{6} =$

G $1\frac{1}{3} + 2\frac{1}{6} =$ $3\frac{1}{2} + 2\frac{2}{5} =$ $4\frac{2}{7} + \frac{9}{14} =$ $3\frac{3}{8} + 2\frac{5}{12} =$

     $\frac{11}{20} + 2\frac{2}{5} =$ $3\frac{5}{16} + 2\frac{3}{8} =$ $2\frac{4}{15} + 3\frac{3}{10} =$ $\frac{3}{4} + 4\frac{1}{5} =$

H $2\frac{7}{10} + 3\frac{11}{15} =$ $3\frac{6}{7} + 2\frac{11}{14} =$ $4\frac{4}{5} + 3\frac{3}{4} =$ $6\frac{1}{2} + 3\frac{11}{12} =$

     $4\frac{2}{3} + 1\frac{7}{8} =$ $1\frac{19}{20} + 4\frac{7}{10} =$ $8\frac{3}{24} + 2\frac{11}{12} =$ $5\frac{3}{4} + 4\frac{7}{12} =$

I $\frac{1}{3} + \frac{1}{6} + \frac{7}{12} =$ $\frac{5}{8} + \frac{7}{24} + \frac{3}{12} =$ $\frac{3}{10} + \frac{9}{20} + \frac{7}{15} =$

     $2\frac{1}{2} + \frac{3}{4} + 1\frac{3}{5} =$ $1\frac{7}{10} + 2\frac{2}{5} + \frac{7}{20} =$ $4\frac{3}{5} + 2\frac{7}{10} + 1\frac{8}{15} =$

Subtraction of fractions

A $\frac{2}{3} - \frac{1}{3} =$ $\frac{4}{5} - \frac{2}{5} =$ $\frac{9}{10} - \frac{7}{10} =$ $\frac{19}{20} - \frac{13}{20} =$

$\frac{11}{15} - \frac{7}{15} =$ $\frac{19}{30} - \frac{11}{30} =$ $\frac{11}{12} - \frac{5}{12} =$ $\frac{13}{16} - \frac{9}{16} =$

B $\frac{7}{10} - \frac{2}{5} =$ $\frac{3}{4} - \frac{7}{12} =$ $\frac{19}{20} - \frac{4}{5} =$ $\frac{2}{3} - \frac{5}{12} =$

$\frac{15}{16} - \frac{5}{8} =$ $\frac{6}{7} - \frac{9}{14} =$ $\frac{8}{15} - \frac{1}{5} =$ $\frac{4}{5} - \frac{13}{20} =$

C $\frac{3}{4} - \frac{1}{6} =$ $\frac{4}{5} - \frac{3}{4} =$ $\frac{1}{2} - \frac{2}{9} =$ $\frac{7}{8} - \frac{7}{12} =$

$\frac{2}{3} - \frac{5}{8} =$ $\frac{7}{10} - \frac{7}{15} =$ $\frac{2}{3} - \frac{1}{2} =$ $\frac{9}{10} - \frac{3}{4} =$

D $1 - \frac{3}{4} =$ $1 - \frac{7}{8} =$ $1 - \frac{5}{6} =$ $1 - \frac{11}{12} =$

$3 - \frac{15}{16} =$ $5 - \frac{19}{20} =$ $7 - \frac{13}{15} =$ $4 - \frac{13}{14} =$

E $1\frac{7}{8} - \frac{1}{2} =$ $3\frac{3}{4} - \frac{2}{5} =$ $1\frac{19}{20} - \frac{7}{10} =$ $6\frac{2}{3} - \frac{5}{12} =$

$1\frac{14}{15} - \frac{7}{10} =$ $3\frac{11}{16} - \frac{1}{2} =$ $2\frac{14}{15} - \frac{4}{5} =$ $7\frac{1}{2} - \frac{7}{16} =$

F $4\frac{5}{8} - 3\frac{1}{4} =$ $6\frac{7}{10} - 3\frac{3}{5} =$ $2\frac{3}{4} - 1\frac{1}{10} =$ $3\frac{1}{2} - 2\frac{9}{20} =$

$8\frac{4}{5} - 3\frac{7}{15} =$ $4\frac{5}{6} - 2\frac{3}{4} =$ $4\frac{7}{10} - 2\frac{1}{15} =$ $5\frac{8}{9} - 2\frac{2}{3} =$

G $6 - 3\frac{3}{4} =$ $5 - 2\frac{7}{8} =$ $4 - 3\frac{11}{12} =$ $8 - 5\frac{7}{10} =$

$2 - 1\frac{9}{20} =$ $8 - 3\frac{15}{16} =$ $7 - 4\frac{8}{9} =$ $3 - 1\frac{13}{15} =$

H $2\frac{1}{2} - 1\frac{7}{10} =$ $4\frac{1}{3} - 2\frac{5}{12} =$ $8\frac{3}{16} - 4\frac{5}{8} =$ $5\frac{3}{5} - 4\frac{3}{4} =$

$7\frac{1}{10} - 4\frac{2}{3} =$ $9\frac{5}{24} - 3\frac{7}{12} =$ $7\frac{3}{5} - \frac{19}{20} =$ $4\frac{3}{4} - 2\frac{5}{6} =$

I $6\frac{1}{5} - 2\frac{9}{10} =$ $8 - 3\frac{5}{6} =$ $7\frac{1}{2} - \frac{11}{12} =$ $2\frac{9}{10} - 1\frac{4}{5} =$

$9\frac{1}{3} - 2\frac{5}{9} =$ $2\frac{7}{8} - 1\frac{11}{24} =$ $4\frac{11}{15} - 2\frac{9}{10} =$ $2\frac{11}{16} - \frac{7}{8} =$

Multiplication of fractions

A Cancel to lowest terms.

$\frac{15}{20} =$　　$\frac{12}{18} =$　　$\frac{12}{20} =$　　$\frac{9}{12} =$　　$\frac{14}{24} =$　　$\frac{18}{36} =$　　$\frac{24}{30} =$　　$\frac{40}{50} =$　　$\frac{16}{20} =$　　$\frac{30}{40} =$

$\frac{12}{16} =$　　$\frac{10}{20} =$　　$\frac{10}{15} =$　　$\frac{32}{40} =$　　$\frac{16}{18} =$　　$\frac{5}{20} =$　　$\frac{24}{36} =$　　$\frac{20}{25} =$　　$\frac{8}{12} =$　　$\frac{35}{40} =$

B　$\frac{5}{16} \times 3 =$　　　　$\frac{2}{9} \times 4 =$　　　　$\frac{1}{6} \times 5 =$　　　　$\frac{3}{20} \times 3 =$

　　$\frac{2}{11} \times 5 =$　　　　$\frac{3}{16} \times 5 =$　　　　$\frac{2}{5} \times 2 =$　　　　$\frac{1}{12} \times 7 =$

C Give your answers as mixed numbers in lowest terms.

　$\frac{3}{5} \times 6 =$　　　　$\frac{5}{6} \times 3 =$　　　　$\frac{7}{8} \times 4 =$　　　　$\frac{3}{10} \times 8 =$

　$\frac{3}{8} \times 6 =$　　　　$\frac{5}{16} \times 4 =$　　　　$\frac{2}{7} \times 8 =$　　　　$\frac{4}{9} \times 3 =$

D Cancel then multiply the following.

　$\frac{2}{5} \times \frac{1}{2} =$　　　　$\frac{6}{7} \times \frac{2}{3} =$　　　　$\frac{8}{9} \times \frac{3}{5} =$　　　　$\frac{11}{12} \times \frac{4}{7} =$

　$\frac{9}{10} \times \frac{5}{6} =$　　　　$\frac{15}{16} \times \frac{4}{5} =$　　　　$\frac{7}{18} \times \frac{9}{14} =$　　　　$\frac{10}{11} \times \frac{2}{15} =$

E　$1\frac{1}{5} \times 1\frac{1}{3} =$　　　$1\frac{5}{7} \times 1\frac{5}{9} =$　　　$1\frac{1}{8} \times 1\frac{5}{6} =$　　　$1\frac{3}{5} \times 1\frac{1}{4} =$

　　$1\frac{1}{20} \times 1\frac{3}{7} =$　　　$1\frac{3}{25} \times 1\frac{1}{14} =$　　　$1\frac{1}{2} \times 1\frac{1}{3} =$　　　$1\frac{1}{4} \times 1\frac{1}{15} =$

F　$3\frac{1}{3} \times 2\frac{5}{8} =$　　　$3\frac{3}{10} \times 5\frac{5}{6} =$　　　$2\frac{1}{2} \times 1\frac{7}{15} =$　　　$6\frac{3}{4} \times 2\frac{2}{9} =$

　　$2\frac{6}{7} \times 2\frac{4}{5} =$　　　$3\frac{1}{8} \times 2\frac{3}{10} =$　　　$3\frac{3}{4} \times 3\frac{3}{5} =$　　　$3\frac{3}{8} \times 5\frac{1}{3} =$

G　$3\frac{1}{2}$ of $6\frac{6}{7} =$　　　$2\frac{2}{3}$ of $1\frac{5}{16} =$　　　$3\frac{1}{6}$ of $1\frac{4}{5} =$　　　$2\frac{1}{2}$ of $1\frac{1}{3} =$

　　$\frac{2}{3}$ of $1\frac{1}{2} =$　　　$\frac{4}{5}$ of $4\frac{1}{6} =$　　　$3\frac{3}{8}$ of $2\frac{2}{3} =$　　　$4\frac{7}{12}$ of $2\frac{2}{11} =$

Division of fractions

A $\frac{4}{5} \div 2 =$ $\frac{9}{10} \div 3 =$ $\frac{6}{7} \div 2 =$ $\frac{15}{16} \div 5 =$

     $\frac{9}{16} \div 3 =$ $\frac{6}{11} \div 2 =$ $\frac{8}{9} \div 8 =$ $\frac{24}{25} \div 6 =$

B $1\frac{2}{5} \div 7 =$ $2\frac{2}{7} \div 8 =$ $4\frac{1}{5} \div 3 =$ $6\frac{3}{4} \div 9 =$

     $3\frac{1}{3} \div 5 =$ $7\frac{1}{2} \div 3 =$ $2\frac{2}{9} \div 10 =$ $8\frac{1}{4} \div 11 =$

C $4 \div \frac{1}{3} =$ $6 \div \frac{1}{7} =$ $5 \div \frac{1}{12} =$ $4 \div \frac{1}{6} =$

     $6 \div \frac{3}{10} =$ $8 \div \frac{4}{5} =$ $12 \div \frac{15}{16} =$ $9 \div \frac{9}{10} =$

D $8 \div 1\frac{3}{5} =$ $7 \div 2\frac{1}{10} =$ $6 \div 2\frac{1}{4} =$ $15 \div 2\frac{1}{12} =$

     $2 \div 1\frac{1}{3} =$ $4 \div 3\frac{1}{3} =$ $9 \div 2\frac{7}{10} =$ $5 \div 3\frac{3}{4} =$

E $\frac{4}{5} \div \frac{7}{15} =$ $\frac{7}{8} \div \frac{11}{16} =$ $\frac{11}{12} \div \frac{5}{6} =$ $\frac{14}{15} \div \frac{7}{10} =$

     $\frac{7}{20} \div \frac{7}{15} =$ $\frac{3}{4} \div \frac{15}{16} =$ $\frac{11}{25} \div \frac{11}{15} =$ $\frac{9}{10} \div \frac{7}{30} =$

F $\frac{11}{12} \div 1\frac{1}{10} =$ $\frac{5}{6} \div 3\frac{3}{4} =$ $\frac{17}{20} \div 1\frac{7}{10} =$ $\frac{14}{15} \div 2\frac{4}{5} =$

     $\frac{12}{25} \div 2\frac{4}{5} =$ $\frac{11}{18} \div 2\frac{2}{9} =$ $\frac{7}{8} \div 3\frac{1}{2} =$ $\frac{3}{10} \div 1\frac{4}{5} =$

G $4\frac{1}{8} \div \frac{3}{4} =$ $3\frac{1}{3} \div \frac{4}{7} =$ $2\frac{5}{6} \div 1\frac{1}{16} =$ $8\frac{2}{5} \div \frac{7}{15} =$

     $1\frac{4}{9} \div \frac{13}{15} =$ $3\frac{1}{2} \div \frac{7}{8} =$ $2\frac{1}{2} \div \frac{5}{6} =$ $2\frac{1}{12} \div \frac{5}{6} =$

H $2\frac{4}{9} \div 3\frac{2}{3} =$ $1\frac{5}{7} \div 1\frac{1}{14} =$ $3\frac{3}{5} \div 1\frac{11}{16} =$ $1\frac{5}{16} \div 1\frac{1}{20} =$

     $5\frac{7}{9} \div 8\frac{2}{3} =$ $3\frac{3}{4} \div 3\frac{3}{8} =$ $6\frac{3}{5} \div 1\frac{1}{10} =$ $2\frac{5}{6} \div 1\frac{1}{16} =$

     $3\frac{2}{3} \div 4\frac{1}{8} =$ $2\frac{5}{8} \div 3\frac{1}{9} =$ $2\frac{2}{9} \div 2\frac{11}{12} =$ $2\frac{7}{10} \div 1\frac{11}{25} =$

Fractional parts

A Complete:

$\frac{4}{5}$ of 60p = $\frac{3}{4}$ of 100 g= $\frac{7}{8}$ of 56 = $\frac{9}{10}$ of 50 m =

$\frac{5}{6}$ of £2·40= $\frac{11}{12}$ of 240= $\frac{5}{8}$ of 816= $\frac{5}{16}$ of 320 km =

$\frac{9}{20}$ of 400 g = $\frac{7}{8}$ of 96 = $\frac{27}{100}$ of £1·00 = $\frac{4}{5}$ of 25 kg =

$\frac{3}{4}$ of 80p= $\frac{3}{8}$ of 144 = $\frac{2}{3}$ of 387 = $\frac{19}{20}$ of £600·00 =

$\frac{11}{12}$ of 120 cm = $\frac{7}{10}$ of 1000= $\frac{5}{7}$ of £2·73 = $\frac{4}{15}$ of 450 km =

$\frac{7}{15}$ of £90·00 = $\frac{5}{9}$ of 81 g = $\frac{8}{11}$ of 341 g = $\frac{7}{10}$ of 500 g =

$\frac{9}{30}$ of 3000 = $\frac{5}{12}$ of 276 km = $\frac{3}{7}$ of 350 m = $\frac{9}{16}$ of £4·80 =

B Find the whole when:

$\frac{1}{3}$ is 50p $\frac{1}{5}$ is 24 g $\frac{1}{7}$ is 35 m $\frac{1}{6}$ is 20 l

$\frac{3}{4}$ is 45p $\frac{4}{5}$ is 84 $\frac{6}{7}$ is £42·00 $\frac{2}{3}$ is 120 km

$\frac{1}{2}$ is £7·50 $\frac{5}{8}$ is 625 g $\frac{7}{10}$ is 140 $\frac{4}{5}$ is £1·20

$\frac{9}{20}$ is 270 m $\frac{11}{15}$ is £3·63 $\frac{5}{6}$ is 100 kg $\frac{7}{12}$ is 56

C Express as fractions in lowest terms.

50 of 100   75 of 100   60 of 80   125 of 250

Decimal notation

A Write as decimals.

1 $\frac{7}{100}$ $\frac{9}{10}$ $\frac{1}{10}$ $\frac{15}{100}$ $\frac{13}{100}$ $\frac{4}{100}$ $\frac{3}{10}$ $\frac{6}{10}$ $\frac{63}{100}$ $\frac{11}{100}$

2 nineteen hundredths   six hundredths

two tenths   twenty-one hundredths

two hundredths   eight tenths

3 eighteen tenths   one hundred and forty-one hundredths

twenty-five tenths   one unit and eight hundredths

one hundred and forty-six tenths   two hundred and twenty-nine hundredths

4 $4\frac{7}{100}$ $3\frac{9}{10}$ $6\frac{14}{100}$ $8\frac{7}{10}$ $9\frac{3}{100}$ $11\frac{43}{100}$ $12\frac{63}{100}$ $4\frac{1}{10}$

B Write the value of the underlined figure in words.

627·4<u>3</u>   1<u>8</u>·21   4·0<u>7</u>   <u>1</u>41·31   <u>4</u>216·9

6050·0<u>2</u>   <u>3</u>6·21   <u>4</u>71·82   101·4<u>5</u>   2<u>8</u>1·06

C **1** 42·6 × 10   3·26 × 100   0·25 × 100   11·27 × 10   4·6 × 100

35·26 × 10   32·45 × 100   0·01 × 10   2·06 × 100   45·1 × 100

2 42·7 ÷ 10   136·00 ÷ 100   11·2 ÷ 10   1432 ÷ 100   14·6 ÷ 10

0·2 ÷ 10   2·00 ÷ 100   1471 ÷ 100   6·6 ÷ 10   243 ÷ 100

D How many tenths in:

1 2·1?   3·0?   0·7?   14·3?   4·9?   16·0?   0·3?   12·4?

2 How many hundredths in:

0·23?   4·06?   2·30?   0·07?   4·27?   3·26?   0·09?   0·11?

Decimal notation

A Write as decimals.

1 $\frac{4}{1000}$ $\frac{16}{1000}$ $\frac{216}{1000}$ $\frac{19}{1000}$ $\frac{2}{1000}$ $\frac{303}{1000}$ $\frac{43}{1000}$ $\frac{21}{1000}$

2 twenty-five thousandths   one hundred and one thousandths

   fourteen thousandths   eight thousandths

   sixteen thousandths   two hundred and fifty thousandths

B Write the number of thousandths in:

0·007   0·016   0·12   0·436   0·82   0·009

0·125   0·027   0·36   0·207   0·005   0·75

C Arrange each line in order of size. Begin with the greatest.

43·00   4·3   0·43   0·043   4·003   40·03

11·02   11·002   1·102   1·012   11·2   1·12

90·01   9·01   0·901   91·0   0·091   0·91

D **1** Multiply each number by 1000.

2·4   0·261   5·0   4·01   3·006   6·27   3·415   2·6

2 Divide each number by 1000.

4231   41   321   6   12   3421   18   106

E What must be done to the 5 in the number 0·0$\underline{5}$0 to make it worth:

a 5 tenths?   **b** 5 tens?   **c** 5 hundreds?   **d** 5 hundredths?

e 5 thousandths?   **f** 5 thousands?   **g** 5 ones?

F **1** 4·2 × 1000   3·45 × 10   0·41 × 1000   0·11 × 10   0·01 × 100

2 2641 ÷ 1000   2·6 ÷ 100   0·06 ÷ 10   27·00 ÷ 1000   0·01 ÷ 10

Decimals – addition and subtraction

A

$1 \cdot 6 + 0 \cdot 125 + 16 \cdot 32 =$

$214 \cdot 3 + 18 \cdot 271 + 8 \cdot 279 =$

$32 \cdot 26 + 0 \cdot 714 + 314 \cdot 283 =$

$8 \cdot 01 + 19 \cdot 245 + 0 \cdot 076 =$

$28 \cdot 376 + 0 \cdot 009 + 7 \cdot 26 =$

$24 \cdot 04 + 3 \cdot 269 + 24 \cdot 009 =$

$88 \cdot 261 + 0 \cdot 384 + 5 \cdot 2 =$

$54 \cdot 021 + 1271 \cdot 2 + 0 \cdot 099 =$

$29 \cdot 351 + 18 \cdot 206 + 1721 \cdot 087 =$

$435 + 2 \cdot 088 + 26 \cdot 79 =$

B Set down as decimals and then add.

$3 \frac{7}{10} + 14 \frac{19}{1000} + 214 \frac{109}{1000}$

$19 \frac{3}{10} + 21 \frac{13}{1000} + 41 \frac{7}{100}$

$54 \frac{7}{100} + 26 \frac{11}{1000} + 8 \frac{3}{10}$

$99 \frac{13}{1000} + 41 \frac{6}{10} + 8 \frac{119}{1000}$

$14 \frac{1}{1000} + 104 \frac{14}{1000} + 2 \frac{3}{100}$

$\frac{16}{100} + 4 \frac{8}{100} + 11 \frac{145}{1000}$

$21 \frac{1}{100} + \frac{436}{1000} + 214 \frac{17}{1000}$

$\frac{72}{1000} + \frac{145}{1000} + 126 \frac{3}{100}$

$2 \frac{7}{10} + 18 \frac{13}{100} + 4 \frac{216}{1000}$

$12 \frac{2}{100} + 16 \frac{17}{1000} + \frac{216}{1000}$

C Subtract the smaller from the greater in each pair of numbers.

$4 \cdot 27$ and $5 \cdot 26$		$12 \cdot 43$ and $12 \cdot 078$
$0 \cdot 99$ and $0 \cdot 099$		$18 \cdot 06$ and $19 \cdot 11$
$3 \cdot 026$ and $3 \cdot 1$		$23 \cdot 006$ and $23 \cdot 1$
$216 \cdot 43$ and $216 \cdot 053$		$214 \cdot 06$ and $214 \cdot 006$
$9 \cdot 6$ and $8 \cdot 216$		$326 \cdot 45$ and $429 \cdot 009$

D Set down as decimals and then subtract.

$14 \frac{3}{10} - 7 \frac{19}{100} =$

$204 \frac{17}{1000} - 81 \frac{125}{1000} =$

$144 \frac{1}{10} - 76 \frac{17}{100} =$

$12 \frac{216}{1000} - 7 \frac{15}{100} =$

$202 \frac{14}{100} - 201 \frac{99}{1000} =$

$60 \frac{54}{1000} - \frac{999}{1000} =$

$841 \frac{1}{100} - 632 \frac{72}{1000} =$

$279 \frac{13}{1000} - 85 \frac{3}{10} =$

Decimals – multiplication and division

A **1** $0.07 \times 4 =$ $0.3 \times 6 =$ $0.8 \times 5 =$ $0.005 \times 3 =$

      $0.7 \times 6 =$ $0.003 \times 5 =$ $0.4 \times 7 =$ $0.09 \times 9 =$

      $0.017 \times 2 =$ $0.08 \times 8 =$

2 $0.14 \times 6 =$ $0.013 \times 9 =$ $0.24 \times 5 =$ $0.39 \times 7 =$

      $0.025 \times 8 =$ $0.56 \times 4 =$ $0.82 \times 3 =$ $0.022 \times 9 =$

3

2·4	4·8	5·2	7·7	3·2	6·5
×5	×7	×4	×6	×9	×8

3·14	4·08	6·72	8·09	9·24	3·27
×2	×5	×9	×8	×6	×7

4

1·145	2·071	6·033	9·209	4·009
×3	×5	×8	×9	×7

5·105	8·131	7·209	0·745	0·982
×2	×4	×6	×9	×8

B **1** $9.6 \div 12$ $3.6 \div 6$ $7.2 \div 8$

      $0.54 \div 9$ $0.64 \div 8$ $0.55 \div 5$

      $2.4 \div 3$ $8.8 \div 11$

      $0.48 \div 4$ $0.49 \div 7$

2 $3\overline{)0.42}$ $5\overline{)0.65}$ $9\overline{)0.18}$ $4\overline{)0.76}$ $2\overline{)0.96}$

3 $12\overline{)1.80}$ $7\overline{)2.24}$ $6\overline{)5.04}$ $9\overline{)4.68}$ $8\overline{)7.52}$

4 $2\overline{)7.12}$ $9\overline{)12.87}$ $5\overline{)16.25}$ $4\overline{)18.24}$ $11\overline{)34.21}$

      $12\overline{)65.04}$ $6\overline{)38.94}$ $7\overline{)29.61}$ $8\overline{)36.32}$ $3\overline{)29.61}$

5 $12\overline{)1.704}$ $8\overline{)6.504}$ $9\overline{)4.698}$ $3\overline{)2.391}$ $7\overline{)4.396}$

      $11\overline{)6.765}$ $4\overline{)6.696}$ $5\overline{)8.435}$ $6\overline{)9.852}$ $2\overline{)3.152}$

Approximations

A **1** Approximate these numbers to the nearest ten.

146   273   469   738   621   547   342   844

2 Approximate these numbers to the nearest hundred.

3425   6354   7827   11 768   2986   1672

14 961   4845   9748   9306   12 412   8539

3 Approximate these numbers to the nearest thousand.

14 261   32 581   26 841   19 708   8154

31 076   54 980   62 354   82 451   72 654

4 Approximate these numbers to the nearest tenth.

43·21   124·56   9·24   88·78   62·95

47·42   125·63   22·72   90·47   89·99

5 Approximate these numbers to the nearest whole one.

18·75   45·18   33·86   102·98   22·36   44·73

12·05   82·45   131·55   89·67   129·27   55·50

6 Approximate these numbers to the nearest hundredth.

33·356   82·172   15·177   81·144   68·351

66·215   44·164   222·378   54·279   77·283

B Approximate these numbers to the nearest: **a** whole one **b** ten **c** hundred **d** thousand.

1 15 473·6   **2** 23 627·9   **3** 88 459·3   **4** 102 653·7

5 18 752·8   **6** 32 816·5   **7** 21 433·4   **8** 72 999·9

Percentages

A   What percentage of each square is: **a** shaded?   **b** unshaded?

Write your answer like this.

    1   **a** 22 squares out of 100 = $\frac{22}{100}$ = 22% is shaded.

          b 78 squares out of 100 = $\frac{78}{100}$ = 78% is unshaded.

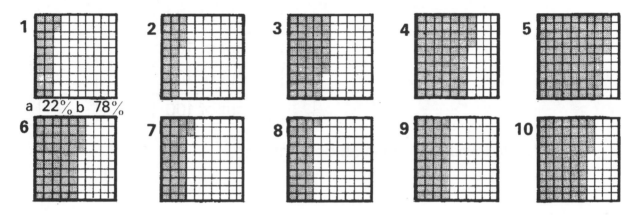

a 22% b 78%

B   There are 100 tiles on this floor.
What percentage of tiles are:

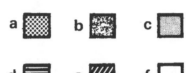

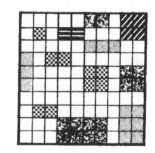

C   The marks scored by the children in the tests were each out of 100. Write
each child's three marks as: **a** a fraction   **b** a percentage.

You do not need to simplify your fractions.

name	English	**a**	**b**	Maths	**a**	**b**	History	**a**	**b**
Anni	47			98			86		
Connor	49			47			99		
Jake	73			82			75		
Jess	86			78			44		
Emily	94			91			96		
Mo	35			74			82		
Naz	90			67			84		
Paul	81			97			41		
Mark	74			98			97		
Chloe	66			88			96		

Percentages

A Complete the table.

$\frac{1}{2}$	50 out of 100	$\frac{50}{100}$	0·50	50%
$\frac{1}{4}$	out of 100			
$\frac{1}{5}$	out of 100			
$\frac{1}{8}$	out of 100			
$\frac{1}{10}$	out of 100			
$\frac{1}{20}$	out of 100			
$\frac{1}{25}$	out of 100			
$\frac{1}{50}$	out of 100			

B Write the following fractions as percentages.

$\frac{3}{4}$ $\frac{4}{5}$ $\frac{3}{10}$ $\frac{7}{25}$ $\frac{17}{50}$ $\frac{11}{25}$ $\frac{13}{20}$ $\frac{7}{8}$ $\frac{3}{5}$ $\frac{5}{8}$ $\frac{11}{50}$ $\frac{7}{20}$

$\frac{49}{50}$ $\frac{19}{25}$ $\frac{2}{5}$ $\frac{9}{20}$ $\frac{43}{50}$ $\frac{3}{25}$ $\frac{24}{25}$ $\frac{33}{50}$ $\frac{19}{20}$ $\frac{23}{50}$ $\frac{7}{10}$ $\frac{9}{10}$

C Write as fractions in lowest terms.

25%   72%   30%   60%   75%   29%   88%   90%   16%   35%

18%   66%   13%   85%   62%   45%   80%   70%   76%   32%

D

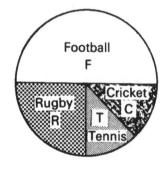

Boys' favourite sports

1 What fraction of the boys like each sport?

2 What percentage like each sport?

3 If there are 40 boys in the class, how many like:

    a football?   **b** rugby?   **c** tennis?

    d cricket?

E

name	shots	goals	%
Freya	25	21	
Holly	10	9	
Frances	16	12	
Mia	20	17	
Evie	12	6	

Netball practice

1 Complete the table to show the percentage of accurate shots.

2 How many times did each girl miss?

3 Write the misses of each girl as a percentage.

Percentages

A 1 What percentage of £1·00 is:

20p?   7p?   25p?   36p?   27p?   32p?   72p?   85p?

2 What percentage of 1 metre is:

35 cm? $22\frac{1}{2}$ cm?   74 cm?   63 cm?   20 mm?   60 mm?

3 What percentage of a kg is:

200 g?   400 g?   700 g?   40 g?   50 g?   250 g?   750 g?

B 1 Express the following: **a** as a fraction   **b** as a percentage.

You do not need to simplify your fractions.

35 of 50	20 of 200	56 of 100	15 of 20
25 of 250	36 of 50	9 of 36	15 of 60
21 of 105	90 of 250	32 of 50	12 of 25

2 Find:

5% of £1·00	£3·00	£7·00	£7·20	£9·40
25% of £1·00	£4·60	£6·80	£9·60	£10·20
8% of £1·00	£16·00	£24·00	£30·00	£45·00

C Find the value of:

10% of 70p	5% of 50 m	1% of £3·00
20% of 90	$12\frac{1}{2}$ % of 72 g	100% of 99
20% of 250 kg	75% of 60	2% of 75 mm
4% of £3·00	5% of 1000	25% of 240

D Find the value of:

a	10%	30%	70%	90%	of 80 kg
b	20%	40%	60%	80%	of 350 m
c	5%	15%	25%	35%	of 200 g
d	4%	8%	12%	16%	of 325 l

Capacity – notation

A

1 Change to millilitres.

0·275 l   3·629 l   2·530 l   5·036 l   0·052 l

4·326 l   0·007 l   8·040 l   6·271 l   10·130 l

2 Change to litres.

3269 ml   629 ml   2014 ml   16 141 ml   2130 ml

14 321 ml   76 ml   127 ml   520 ml   26 ml

3 Change to a decimal fraction and then to ml.
Example: $3\frac{2}{5}$ l = 3·4 l = 3400 ml

$2\frac{1}{5}$ l $3\frac{3}{4}$ l $\frac{9}{10}$ l $4\frac{1}{2}$ l $6\frac{4}{5}$ l $2\frac{1}{4}$ l $5\frac{3}{10}$ l $1\frac{3}{5}$ l

4 By how much is each of these volumes less than $\frac{1}{2}$ l?

325 ml   492 ml   154 ml   261ml   196 ml   421 ml

5 By how much is each of these volumes more than $\frac{3}{4}$ l?

843 ml   961 ml   763 ml   892 ml   993 ml   781 ml

B

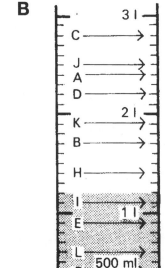

1 How many ml could this container hold?

2 What does each small gradation represent?

3 Write in ml what quantity is represented by each letter on the scale.

4 Write each of your answers to question 3 as:
a a decimal fraction   **b** a fraction of a litre.

5 How much liquid is in the container?

6 How much more liquid would be needed to make it up to:
a $1\frac{1}{2}$ l?   **b** 2 l?   **c** $2\frac{1}{2}$ l?   **d** 3 l?

Capacity – addition and subtraction

A 1 Copy and complete with > or < or =.

1·2 l	1241 ml	3·400 l	$3\frac{2}{5}$ l	807 ml	0·087 l
$\frac{3}{4}$ l	752 ml	2·150 l	2050 ml	8·070 l	870 ml
0·6 l	575 ml	50 ml	0·050 l	$\frac{3}{4}$ l	0·600 l
0·9 l	892 ml	800 ml	$\frac{4}{5}$ l	3·261 l	3621 ml

2 Write each of these to the nearest litre.

2·437 l   3 l 670 ml   5230 ml   7941 ml $3\frac{9}{10}$ l

4 l 271 ml   16·741 l   897 ml $3\frac{4}{5}$ l   6 l 945 ml

3 Write each of these to the nearest $\frac{1}{2}$ litre.

2471 ml   2 l 230 ml   721 ml   3249 ml   4 l 530 ml

3427 ml   4·293 l   7980 ml   5 l 870 ml   61 270 ml

B 1 How much must be added to each of the following to make them up to:

a 1 l?   **b** $1\frac{1}{2}$ l?   **c** 2 l?

230 ml   650 ml   380 ml   191 ml   320 ml   962 ml

55 ml   332 ml   754 ml   909 ml   621 ml   451 ml

2 Subtract the smaller from the greater and give the answer in ml.

a 1 l 45 ml and 1045 ml   **b** 3241 ml and 3 l 240 ml

c 4·026 l and $4\frac{3}{4}$ l   **d** 2170 ml and 2·710 l

C What is the total capacity in: **a** litres   **b** millilitres of the following jars?

1 2 one-litre and 3 half-litre jars

2 12 half-litre and 5 250-millilitre jars

3 3 one-litre, 3 half-litre and 3 250-millilitre jars

Mass

A What is the total weight in each of these?

50g + 150g + 500g + 900g =   75g + 125g + 350g + 400g =

200g + 250g + 100g + 750g =   450g + 500g + 750g +   10g =

200g + 600g + 400g + 150g =   600g + 300g + 150g +   50g =

300g + 250g + 100g + 200g =   900g + 450g + 350g + 140g =

B Write the following in kg.

1   300 g   700 g   50 g   75 g   250 g   80 g   950 g   85 g

2   3450 g   1250 g   4320 g   5006 g   7341 g   9220 g

C Write as grams.

1 $\frac{1}{4}$ kg $\frac{3}{5}$ kg $\frac{3}{10}$ kg $\frac{3}{4}$ kg $\frac{2}{5}$ kg $\frac{7}{10}$ kg $\frac{4}{5}$ kg $\frac{1}{10}$ kg $\frac{1}{5}$ kg

2 $1\frac{1}{2}$ kg $3\frac{2}{5}$ kg $4\frac{3}{4}$ kg $6\frac{3}{10}$ kg $8\frac{3}{5}$ kg $7\frac{1}{4}$ kg $2\frac{7}{10}$ kg $4\frac{4}{5}$ kg

3   1·62 kg   0·77 kg   1·46 kg   1·6 kg   3·7 kg   0·7 kg   0·9 kg

D Use the signs > or < to show which is the heavier of these pairs.

$1\frac{3}{4}$ kg   1700 g   0·8 kg   759 g

$2\frac{3}{5}$ kg   2·7 kg   0·006 kg   7 g

0·85 kg   854 g   510 g $\frac{1}{2}$ kg

$\frac{4}{5}$ kg   750 g   1254 g $1\frac{1}{4}$ kg

759 g $\frac{3}{4}$ kg $\frac{9}{10}$ kg   1050 g

Mass

A 1 Write as tonnes and kilograms.

    3216 kg   2141 kg   6020 kg   8025 kg   1416 kg   3219 kg

2 Write as tonnes.

    4126 kg   347 kg   74 kg   92 kg   1146 kg   96 kg   175 kg

3 Write as kilograms.

    0·236 t   0·014 t   6·016 t   0·236 t   8·212 t   0·017 t

4 What is the total weight in tonnes in each of these?

    1·342 t + 346 kg + 2·256 t $1\frac{1}{2}$ t + 436 kg + 0·750 t

    0·321 t + 1426 kg + 0·014 t   416 kg + 359 kg + 6214 kg

    0·401 t + 91 721 kg + 3 t $\frac{3}{4}$ t + 2·56 t + 750 kg

    5·210 t + 0·216 t + 3414 kg   2·154 t + $2\frac{1}{2}$ t + 14 kg

B 1 What is the greatest weight which can be measured on this scale?

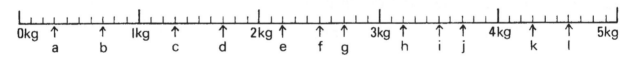

2 Write down the weights indicated by the pointers **a** to **l**.

C

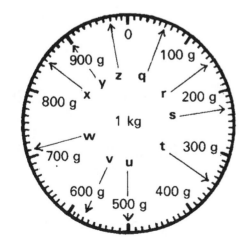

1 What is the greatest weight which can be weighed on the scale?

2 What weight is each small division on the scale worth?

3 What weight is shown by the pointer when it is at points q, r, s, t, u, v, w, x, y and z?

Length

A 1 Change to millimetres.

3026 m $15\frac{2}{5}$ m   6·075 m $3\frac{3}{4}$ m   0·026 m

2 Write in metres.

3241 mm   8186 mm   74 mm   9 mm   147 mm

525 mm   64 mm   4025 mm   6 mm   4396 mm

3 Write in metres.

3·5 km   4·2 km   7·25 km   6·75 km   0·375 km

$6\frac{3}{4}$ km $3\frac{3}{10}$ km $4\frac{4}{5}$ km   1·070 km   3·75 km

4 Write as: **a** kilometres and metres   **b** kilometres.

3250 m   1742 m   1035 m   2072 m   3153 m

4320 m   2065 m   4635 m   4340 m   1007 m

B 1 Write to the nearest centimetre.

326 mm   74 mm   26 mm   814 mm

2 Write to the nearest metre.

2173 cm   1645 cm   2931 cm   5106 cm   4281 cm

0·673 m   4·256 m   6·249 m   7·145 m   3·594 m

3 Write to the nearest kilometre.

4736 m   7141 m   2406 m   8035 m   9025 m

43·276 km   62·759 km   126·475 km   26·157 km   6·325 km

4 Write to the nearest centimetre.

1·473 m   6·296 m   12·431 m   0·726 m   0·683 m

Length

A   **1**   Measure each line in mm.

A _____

B _____

C _____

D _____

E _____

F _____

2   How much longer is:

line E than line A?   line D than line C?

line B than line E?   line A than line F?

line B than line C?   line B than line A?

line D than line F?   line E than line C?

3   Which 2 lines when added are: **a** as long as line A?
                                              b as long as line B?

4   Which would give the greater length?

A + C or D + F   E + C or A + C + F

5   What is the difference in length between:

A + B and E + F?   D + C and B + F?

B   Measure the sides of these shapes in mm, then write: **a** the length
    b the width   **c** the perimeter.

Area and perimeter

Measure the sides of these shapes in cm then find: **a** the perimeter **b** the area.

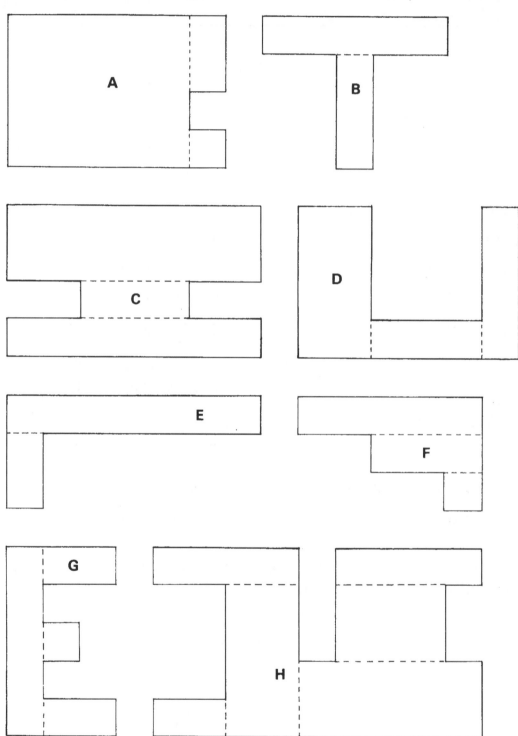

Scale drawing

A **1** Copy and complete. scale: 1 cm to 10 cm

scale length (in cm)	4	6	$8\frac{3}{4}$	$8\frac{1}{2}$	$9\frac{1}{4}$	$5\frac{1}{2}$	12	$6\frac{1}{4}$	10	$7\frac{1}{4}$	$5\frac{1}{4}$	$9\frac{3}{4}$
true length (in cm)												

2 Copy and complete. scale: 1 cm to 25 km

scale length (in cm)												
true length (in km)	100	375	625	150	225	75	500	50	325	425	250	175

3 Copy and complete. scale: $\frac{1}{2}$ cm to 2 cm

scale length (in cm)	$4\frac{1}{2}$		$6\frac{1}{2}$		3	$3\frac{1}{4}$			$9\frac{1}{2}$			10
true length (in cm)		19		52			48	16		23	50	

B Give the real lengths of the sides of these shapes.

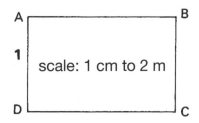

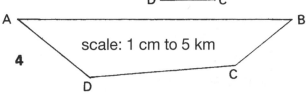

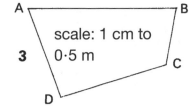

C How long is each street? Scale: 1 cm to 100 m

Ivy St

High St

Walter St

St. Ann St

Green St

Scale drawing

A   What is the real length represented by these lines if the scale is 1 mm to $\frac{1}{2}$ cm?

a _____

b _____

c _____

d _____

e _____

B   **1**   Using a scale of:

   a   1 mm to 2 cm, draw lines to represent:

   46 cm   0·8 m   76 cm   2·4 m   3·6 m   96 cm

   b   1 mm to 5 m, draw lines to represent:

   175 m   240 m   365 m   430 m   600 m   525 m

C   This is the ground floor of a house drawn to a scale of 0·5 cm to 2 m.

Find out the real:

a   length

b   width

c   area of each room.

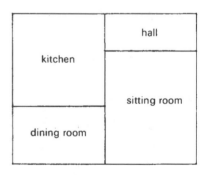

D   This is Isla's bedroom drawn to a scale of 10 mm to 1 m.

Find the real:

a   length and breadth of the (i) room (ii) bed (iii) table (iv) wardrobe

b   width of the (i) window (ii) door.

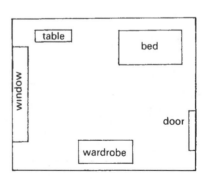

Approximations

A **1** Approximate these measurements to the nearest metre.

3 m 69 cm   15 m 21 cm   18 m 92 cm $3\frac{3}{4}$ m   24 m 59 cm

16·115 m   12·732 m   25·599 m   3·069 m   15·725 m

2 Approximate these measurements to the nearest kilometre.

3 km 800 m   24 km 62 m   33 km 520 m   126 km 274 m $9\frac{1}{4}$ km

14 km 241 m   14·036 km   21·731 km   83·523 km   126·702 km

3 Approximate these weights to the nearest kilogram.

4 kg 270 g   16 kg 750 g   23 kg 532 g   1 kg 84 g   32 kg 147 g

16·027 kg   85·731 kg   54·276 kg   125·808 kg   24·075 kg

4 Approximate these sums of money to the nearest £.

£1·75   £41·32   £62·07   £54·39   £7·69   £8·83

£3·54   £6·73   £26·47   £18·70   £36·09   £54·17

5 Approximate the following to the nearest whole unit.

32·6   £7·21 $3\frac{5}{6}$ 47·39   821·8   4·275 km

20 l 345 ml   7 km 21 m $9\frac{11}{12}$ $8\frac{1}{6}$ 98·43 l   276·95 m

99·9   20 cm 7 mm $45\frac{1}{2}$p   6·035 kg $10\frac{1}{2}$ 41·525 km

B

Liverpool v Everton	55 041
Bolton v Chelsea	34 751
Man. Utd v Tottenham	42 170
Southampton v Norwich	35 496
Aston Villa v Birmingham	40 162
Arsenal v Man. City	39 753

1 Approximate these football crowds to the nearest thousand.

2 Which two crowds approximate to 35 000?

3 Which two crowds approximate to 40 000?

Measures

1 A farmer sells 20 tonnes of potatoes in sacks each holding 25 kg. How many sacks does he need?

2 One litre of ice cream fills 8 tubs. How many tubs are needed for 145 litres of ice-cream?

3 If Eva was 7 cm taller she would be twice as tall as Jade. Jade is 75 cm tall so how tall is Eva?

4 A rectangle has a perimeter of $1\frac{1}{2}$ metres. If the width is 33 cm what is the length?

5 Half a litre of paint costs £1·25. What will be the cost of $4\frac{1}{2}$ litres?

6 A box containing sweets weighs 5 kg. If the box weighs 600 g when it is empty how many 50 g packets of sweets can be made from the contents?

7 How many pieces of card each measuring 8 cm by 10 cm can be cut from a sheet 150 cm × 64 cm?

8 How many bottles each holding 150 ml can be filled from a container holding 6 litres of milk?

9 A grocer received 10 cases of butter. Each case held 20 packets of butter each weighing 250 g. What was the weight of butter in kilograms?

10 If a boy's step is 50 cm, how many metres will he cover in 500 steps?

11 Beef is £2·20 for a kg. What will it cost for:

    a 100 g?   **b** 1·6 kg?   **c** 2·7 kg?

12 A dish holds 780 ml. How many whole litres will 8 dishes hold?

Telling time

A   Write the times shown on these clocks in figures only.

B   Write these times in words like this: 3·42 = 18 minutes to 4.

| 4:45 | 6:26 | 9:32 | 4:05 | 2:12 | 6:56 | 9:45 | 7:21 |

| 1:53 | 4:16 | 8:31 | 3:49 | 5:23 | 10:47 | 11:18 | 12:41 |

C   A clock was 7 minutes slow. What were the real times (in figures) when it showed:

| 6:59? | 9:42? | 3:54? | 10:20? | 12:56? | 11:09? | 10:55? |

| 4:19? | 2:53? | 9:12? | 8:34? | 1:57? | 7:43? | 5:58? |

D   Another clock was 15 minutes fast. What were the real times (in figures) when it showed:

| 7:06? | 6:24? | 9:14? | 11:32? | 10:49? | 2:03? | 8:15? |

| 1:05? | 3:12? | 5:20? | 12:56? | 4:11? | 7:10? | 2:09? |

E   How many minutes are needed to take these times to the next hour?

| 3:45 | 8:32 | 2:53 | 7:14 | 10:09 | 4:23 | 6:07 |

| 1:12 | 9:18 | 11:42 | 5:47 | 6:38 | 8:25 | 12:19 |

Telling time

A 1 Write the time shown on each of these clocks in two ways.

2 Clock A shows the correct time. By how much is each clock fast?

B How many hours and minutes between:

5:30 am and 12:50 pm? 　　　　　 9:32 am and 1:40 pm?

11:18 am and 2:27 pm? 　　　　　 6:45 am and 2:20 pm?

10:52 am and 3:20 pm? 　　　　　 8:10 am and 3:34 pm?

11:49 am and 12:32 pm? 　　　　 10:05 am and 5:04 pm?

C Write down how many minutes there are in:

1

1 h	$\frac{1}{2}$ h	$\frac{1}{4}$ h	$\frac{1}{5}$ h
$\frac{1}{12}$ h	$\frac{1}{6}$ h	$\frac{1}{3}$ h	$\frac{1}{10}$ h
$2\frac{2}{5}$ h	$2\frac{1}{12}$ h	$3\frac{3}{4}$ h	$4\frac{3}{10}$ h
$5\frac{2}{3}$ h	$7\frac{5}{6}$ h	$1\frac{4}{5}$ h	$4\frac{7}{10}$ h
$1\frac{5}{12}$ h	$3\frac{3}{5}$ h	$5\frac{7}{12}$ h	$4\frac{11}{12}$ h

2

1 h 23 min	2 h 46 min	5 h 7 min
9 h 14 min	3 h 16 min	6 h 29 min
4 h 32 min	7 h 4 min	

D Change to hours and minutes.

142 min	76 min	253 min	91 min	132 min	69 min
212 min	83 min	179 min	89 min	345 min	164 min

E How many seconds in:

$2\frac{1}{2}$ min?　　 $3\frac{3}{4}$ min?　　 $8\frac{1}{4}$ min?　　 $4\frac{3}{5}$ min?　　 $5\frac{7}{10}$ min?　　 $6\frac{11}{12}$ min?

Telling time

A 1 Write in words the times shown on these digital clocks.

| 0 7 4 3 | 0 9 1 2 | 1 1 3 2 | 1 0 5 9 | 0 4 3 6 |

| 0 1 2 9 | 0 6 5 3 | 0 8 4 1 | 0 5 5 3 | 1 2 4 7 |

2 Draw digital clocks to show these times.

quarter to ten   twenty-five past six

eight o'clock   thirty-six minutes past nine

forty-seven minutes past three   eighteen minutes to one

five minutes past ten

B 1 Buses leave at 20 minute intervals. Complete the table.

8:55	9:15											

2 A bus journey takes 12 minutes. Complete the table.

depart	8:00	8:15	8:30	8:45	9:00	9:15	9:30	9:45	10:00	10:15	10:30	10:45
arrive	8:12											

C

BBC—Sunday		duration	ITV—Friday		duration
7:15–8:30	Open University		9:30	History Around You	
9:00–9:15	The Flumps		9:55	Plain Sailing	
9:40–10:10	News		10:20	News	
10:50	Volunteers		10:40	Journal	
11:15	The Right to Work		10:55	Kathy's Quiz	
11:40–11:50	On the Move		11:05	A Village	
12:15	News		12:00	Handful of Songs	
1:00–1:30	Farming		12:10–12:30	Weather	

Say how long each programme lasts for: **a** BBC – Sunday
b ITV – Friday.

24 hour clock

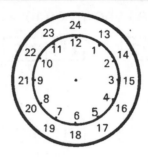

A **1** Rewrite these times in 24 h times.

4:15 am   7:30 am   6:20 am   11:43 am   9:16 am   3:11 am

10:47 am   6:35 am   2:36 am   1:52 am   5:06 am   8:25 am

2 Rewrite these times in 12 h times.

04:12   09:32   08:54   12:29   07:49   08:03

03:51   11:23   05:42   06:07   10:38   01:16

B **1** Rewrite these times in 24 h times.

1:29 pm   4:46 pm   3:34 pm   12:05 pm   10:16 pm   5:12 pm

2:21 pm   11:45 pm   9:38 pm   8:56 pm   6:51 pm   7:09 pm

2 Rewrite these times in 12 h times.

14:41   16:32   23:27   13:23   22:35   19:48

20:56   18:07   15:16   21:51   17:54   16:09

C **1** Rewrite in 24 h times.

1:19 pm   7:07 am   2:46 am   11:25 pm   3:58 pm   10:47 am

12:38 am   4:55 am   8:18 pm   6:02 am   9:33 pm   5:20 pm

2 Rewrite in 12 h times in two ways.

07:09   13:36   04:26   15:19   23:46   06:54

09:49   02:50   18:05   21:23   08:22   20:13

Timetables

A Copy and complete.

journey starts	09:20	17:16	04:11	06:43	15:35	20:16	11:50	21:31
time taken	75 min	46 min	62 min	52 min	49 min	39 min	12 min	22 min
journey ends	10:35							

journey ends	17:00	16:42	20:41	13:14	12:15	16:07	22:12	14:03
journey starts	15:30	13:51	18:52	12:41	07:58	13:20	19:19	03:44
time taken	1 h 30 min							

B Use this bus timetable to answer the following.

Manchester dep.	9:00	9:45	10:30	11:15	12:00	12:45	13:30	14:15
Bolton arr.	9:15		10:45	11:30	12:15		13:45	14:30
Bolton dep.	9:20		10:45	11:35	12:20		13:50	14:35
Chorley arr.	9:40	10:20	11:15	11:55	12:40			14:55
Chorley dep.	9:45	10:25	11:20	12:00	12:40			15:00
Blackpool arr.	10:20	11:00	11:45	12:35	13:15	13:55	14:45	15:35

1 What is the earliest time you could arrive at Blackpool?

2 What is the latest time you can leave Manchester?

3 How long does the quickest bus take?

4 How long are the rest stops at Bolton and Chorley?

5 Which bus picks up at Bolton but does not wait?

6 Which bus picks up at Chorley but does not wait?

7 Which bus calls only at Chorley?

8 Which bus calls only at Bolton?

9 What is the latest time you can leave Bolton to be in Blackpool by 2 o'clock?

10 Jane arrives at Blackpool at 11:00. What time did she leave Chorley?

11 Which buses take 1 h 20 min for the journey?

12 Which buses take 1 h 15 min for the journey?

Calendar

A **1** Write the following dates in numbers only.

15th June 2008	25th October 2007
3rd May 2012	23rd April 2011
25th August 2007	5th February 2008
29th January 2002	20th July 2012
12th March 2010	6th September 2009
20th November 2005	8th December 2011

2 Write these dates in full.

6.2.11	19.7.10	23.4.08	14.8.12	7.3.06	29.9.10
31.1.12	30.6.09	17.10.09	21.5.07	24.12.05	11.11.11

B **1** What will be the date two weeks after the following?

23rd March	30th April	27th June	16th February
16th May	25th September	30th December	25th July

2 What will be the date four weeks after the following?

12th January	26th March	10th August	9th November
20th October	2nd May	25th December	14th January

C **1** How many months from:

1st January 2003 to 1st May 2005?	1st March 2002 to 1st April 2006?
1st February 2009 to 1st January 2011?	1st June 2005 to 1st May 2008?
1st October 2003 to 1st July 2005?	1st November 2001 to 1st April 2009?
1st December 2006 to 1st February 2008?	1st August 2000 to 1st March 2004?

2 How many days are there inclusively between:

4.2.01 and 6.3.01?	15.12.10 and 7.1.11?	3.8.09 and 15.10.09?
11.11.11 and 1.1.12?	9.6.04 and 12.8.04?	16.3.05 and 1.4.05?
30.11.05 and 21.12.05?	25.12.06 and 1.1.07?	17.2.12 and 15.3.12?

Time, speed and distance

1 An athlete runs one lap of a track in 20 s. How long will it take him to run:

2 laps?   4 laps?   5 laps?   3 laps?   6 laps?   10 laps?

2 Jamie walks at 4 km/h. How far will he go in:

1 h?   2 h?   3 h?   4 h? $\frac{1}{2}$ h? $\frac{1}{4}$ h? $\frac{3}{4}$ h? $1\frac{1}{2}$ h? $2\frac{3}{4}$ h?

3 His brother cycles at 12 km/h. How far will he cycle in:

1 h?   2 h?   3 h?   4 h? $\frac{1}{2}$ h? $\frac{1}{4}$ h? $\frac{3}{4}$ h? $\frac{1}{3}$ h? $\frac{2}{3}$ h? $2\frac{3}{4}$ h?

4 What will be the different speeds of a bus if on 5 hour journeys it travels:

180 km?   120 km?   150 km?   90 km?   45 km?   85 km?   65 km?   130 km?

5 What is the speed of each of these cars if they cover these distances in $\frac{1}{2}$ h?
a 20 km   **b** 50 km   **c** 36 km   **d** 80 km   **e** 44 km

6 Travelling at 40 km/h, how long will it take to travel:

120 km?   100 km?   70 km?   90 km?   44 km?   36 km?   24 km?   32 km?

7 A man rows at 10 km/h. How long will it take him to row:

60 km?   45 km?   12 km?   8 km?   24 km?   35 km?   5 km? $7\frac{1}{2}$ km?

Time, speed and distance

A   Copy and complete to show the distance covered.

speed	time					
	1 h	$\frac{1}{2}$ h	$\frac{1}{4}$ h	$\frac{3}{4}$ h	$\frac{1}{3}$ h	$\frac{1}{5}$ h
30 km/h	30 km	15 km	$7\frac{1}{2}$ km	$22\frac{1}{2}$ km	10 km	6 km
60 km/h						
90 km/h						
120 km/h						
150 km/h						

B   Copy and complete to show the time taken.

distance	speed					
	10 km/h	20 km/h	30 km/h	40 km/h	50 km/h	60 km/h
10 km	1 h	30 min	20 min	15 min	12 min	10 min
20 km						
30 km						
40 km						
50 km						

C   Copy and complete to show the speed.

distance	time					
	1 h	$\frac{1}{2}$ h	$\frac{1}{4}$ h	$\frac{3}{4}$ h	$\frac{1}{3}$ h	$\frac{1}{5}$ h
12 km	12 km/h	24 km/h	48 km/h	16 km/h	36 km/h	60 km/h
24 km						
36 km						
48 km						
60 km						

Time, speed and distance

A **1** Find the speed.

time	$1\frac{1}{2}$ h	$2\frac{1}{4}$ h	3 h	$3\frac{1}{2}$ h	4 h
distance	90 km	126 km	156 km	168 km	22 km
speed					

2 Find the distance travelled.

speed	72 km/h	150 km/h	220 km/h	86 km/h	135 km/h
time	$1\frac{1}{3}$ h	2 h 20 min	$2\frac{1}{4}$ h	$\frac{3}{4}$ h	40 min
distance					

3 Find the time taken.

speed	50 km/h	60 km/h	48 km/h	70 km/h	30 km/h
distance	175 km	185 km	84 km	154 km	33 km
time					

B Copy and complete.

vehicle	distance	time	speed
a	100 km	$2\frac{1}{2}$ h	
b		4h	17·5 km/h
c	1500 km		600 km/h
d		$3\frac{1}{4}$ h	90 km/h
e	36 km		27 km/h
f	990 km	3 h 40 min	

Angles

A Use a protractor to measure these angles.

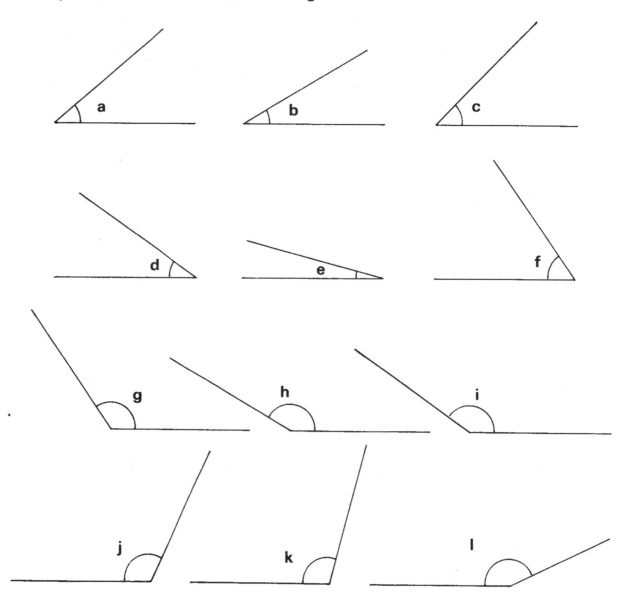

B Use a protractor to draw these angles.

1 45° 75° 85° 10° 20° 35° 70° 50°

2 105° 95° 125° 110° 170° 145° 160° 115°

C **1** Draw and label three acute angles.

2 Draw and label three obtuse angles.

Bearings and direction

A

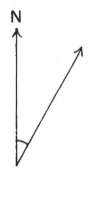

Through how many degrees would you go if you turned:

1	from N to NE?	6	from S to N?
2	from NE to SE?	7	from E to SW?
3	from SE to W?	8	from N to SW?
4	from NW to NE?	9	from S to NW?
5	from W to NE?	10	from SW to SE?

B Write down the following bearings.

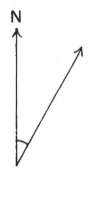
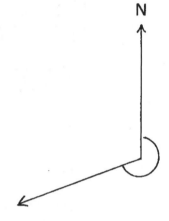

C Give the bearing of each town.

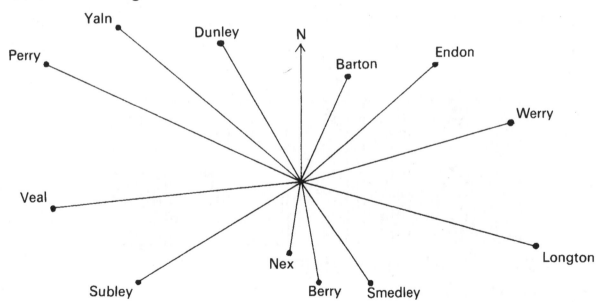

D Plot the following bearings.

1	SW	NE	NW	E	W	SE
2	150°	270°	75°	125°	205°	
	230°	265°	320°	345°	245°	

Block graphs

A

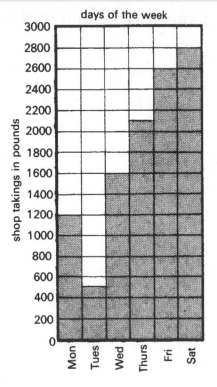

days of the week

shop takings in pounds

1 Which day had the largest takings?

2 Which day had the least takings?

3 What were the total takings for the week?

4 Which day had the same takings as the total takings of Monday and Wednesday?

5 How much more money was taken on Friday than on Tuesday?

6 What was the average takings per day?

7 On which days were the takings more than the average?

8 How much less than the average were the takings on Tuesday?

9 What fraction of the Saturday takings were the Thursday takings?

10 Which day's takings were closest to the average?

B Draw a graph for this table which shows how the children in a school spent their holidays abroad.

Italy	France	Spain	Sweden	Switzerland	Greece	Norway
29	24	37	15	26	7	12

C

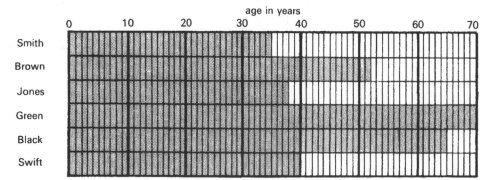

The graph shows the ages of six men.

1 Give the age of each man.

2 How old is the eldest?

3 What is the average age?

4 How old is the youngest?

5 How many of the men are pensioners?

Discontinuous graphs

A

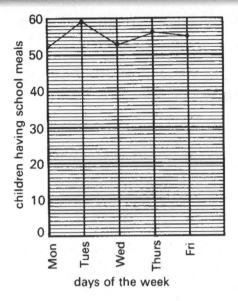

1. On which day did most children stay for lunch?

2. On which day did fewest stay?

3. How many children altogether had lunch during the week?

4. Meals cost £1.00 each. How much dinner money was collected?

5. What was the average number of children per day?

6. On which day did the same number of the children stay as the average?

B Draw the graph for this table which shows the number of accident victims treated in hospital in one week.

Sunday	Monday	Tuesday	Wednesday	Thursday	Friday	Saturday
23	18	21	15	21	35	43

C

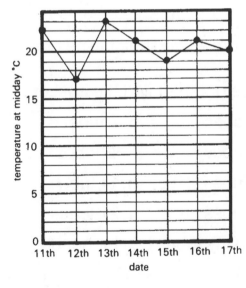

1. Which date had the lowest temperature?

2. Which date had the highest temperature?

3. Which date showed the sharpest increase?

4. Which date showed the sharpest decrease?

5. Which two dates showed the same drop in temperature?

6. What was the difference between the highest and lowest temperatures?

7. Which two dates had the same temperature?

8. How many degrees above freezing was:

   a the highest temperature?

   b the lowest temperature?

D Draw a graph for this table which shows the number of children having birthdays in each month.

Jan	Feb	Mar	Apr	May	June	July	Aug	Sept	Oct	Nov	Dec
11	14	19	2	11	5	—	9	3	13	7	8

Straight line and conversion graphs

A

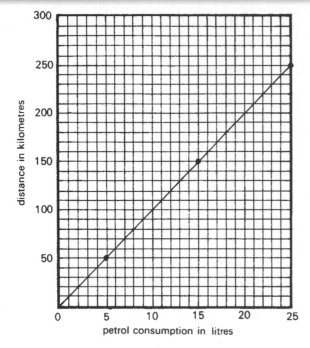

1 What does one small division on the vertical axis represent?

2 How many litres are needed to travel:

   a 50 km?   **b** 150 km?

3 How far could you travel using:

   a 10 l?   **b** 25 l?

   c 17 l?   **d** 23 l?

4 Use the information on the graph to calculate how many kilometres per litre the car does.

5 Calculate the amount of petrol used when travelling:

   a 25 km   **b** 45 km

   c 400 km   **d** 350 km

B **1**

km	24	96	144
time	1 h	4 h	6 h

2

miles	5	15	30
km	8	24	48

Use the information in these two tables to draw two straight line graphs.

C

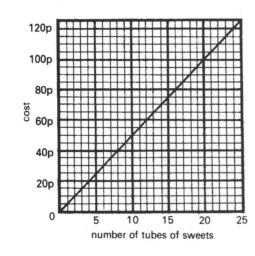

1 Use the graph to find the cost of:

   a 15 tubes   **e** 7 tubes

   b 18 tubes   **f** 12 tubes

   c 22 tubes   **g** 14 tubes

   d 19 tubes   **h** 21 tubes

2 How many tubes can be bought for:

   a 25p?   **c** 95p?   **e** 75p?

   b 85p?   **d** 35p?   **f** 45p?

D Draw two conversion graphs using this information.

1

weight (kg)	1	3	5	10
cost (p)	30	90	150	300

sugar

2

number	2	5	8	9
cost (p)	10	25	40	45

chocolate bars

Answers

Page 2 Addition
A 11, 10, 11, 17, 12;   11, 13, 11, 10, 11;
13, 12, 11, 13, 16;   10, 16, 14, 14, 12;
10, 14, 10, 12, 15;   12, 12, 15, 13, 10;
15, 12, 11, 16, 17;   13, 14, 18, 10, 11;
14, 13, 15, 10, 9
B 65, 119, 105, 133, 117;
101, 80, 118, 113, 192
C 127, 141;   102, 113;   126, 89;
155, 124;   120, 163
D 379, 620, 704, 201, 833;
776, 600, 1077, 419, 895
E 1 351   **2** 975   **3** 271   **4** 245   **5** 1123

Page 3 Addition
A 20, 85, 24, 43, 23;   51, 45, 80, 61, 34;
31, 34, 100, 42, 72;   51, 94, 32, 91, 82;
43, 90, 73, 40, 63;   94, 102, 41, 80, 97;
50, 100, 63, 80, 52;   35, 66, 71, 20, 106;
108, 73, 57, 76, 62
B 2567, 1096, 8978, 8008, 6730;
4302, 3366, 8924, 9998, 9231
C 5258, 8652;   3784, 8520;   9987, 8780;
7835, 9395;   8055, 6623
D 1 2555   **2** 8438   **3** 5734   **4** 4311
5 10 691

Page 4 Subtraction
A 9, 9, 8, 5, 6;   5, 8, 1, 8, 9;   5, 7, 7, 4, 6;
3, 8, 4, 9, 8;   3, 9, 7, 2, 9;   7, 8, 5, 3, 7;
6, 9, 4, 7, 6;   2, 9, 6, 6, 7;   4, 9, 8, 5, 8
B 351, 10, 321, 374, 306;
196, 93, 556, 103, 397
C 153, 263;   594, 473;   372, 201;
518, 194;   395, 251

D

5 0 5	4 6 3	7 7 3	4 2 0	7 4 0
−3 2 9	− 2 7	−2 2 1	−3 5 7	−6 2 9
1 7 6	4 3 6	5 5 2	6 3	1 1 1

7 4 0	5 9 1	4 2 7	8 0 0	5 4 0
−5 3 1	−2 9 6	− 8 6	−1 1 3	−4 3 4
2 0 9	2 9 5	3 4 1	6 8 7	1 0 6

Page 5 Subtraction
A 19, 39, 26, 68, 55;   38, 16, 63, 36, 74;
16, 38, 44, 69, 63;   99, 88, 59, 85, 48;
57, 35, 85, 66, 21;   87, 29, 79, 37, 74;
27, 52, 58, 27, 47;   49, 77, 18, 76, 74;
33, 28, 49, 12, 84

B 121, 3275, 1591, 273, 2483;
2883, 971, 2073, 68, 926
C 3373, 7472;   2544, 2418;   3810, 6638;
4656, 5277;   3106, 5081
D 3296, 188;   88, 2627;   7798, 4686;
7315, 411;   1730, 999
E 1 1070   **2** 2999   **3** 1555   **4** 2881

Page 6 Multiplication
A 4, 21, 60, 36, 54;   18, 20, 48, 30, 10;
40, 0, 8, 6, 36;   66, 36, 15, 33, 25;
18, 44, 32, 12, 28;   48, 0, 50, 24, 9;
16, 30, 0, 35, 14;   72, 24, 22, 60, 16;
45, 20, 27, 0, 0;   24, 55, 42, 40, 12
B 2082, 6355, 8040, 1758, 4596;
3747, 4694, 7080, 3196, 5256
C 6042, 4635, 8284;   6824, 5256, 9297;
3054, 3741, 10 032;   8576, 4876, 8820
D 8292, 8715;   5214, 8046
E 2700, 880

Page 7 Multiplication
A 0, 99, 18, 56, 24;   48, 80, 21, 0, 120;
108, 49, 144, 36, 0;   121, 72, 45, 40, 96;
36, 44 , 64, 63, 77;   32, 54, 14, 90, 72;
84, 35, 132, 22, 0;   81, 18, 48, 60, 66;
55, 0, 27, 88, 70;   16, 110, 42, 28, 33
B 15 197, 51 912, 15 741, 32 056, 23 166;
66 550, 33 669, 60 240, 25 640, 13 923
C 17 168, 49 932, 8487;   35 700, 57 640,
14 940;   22 239, 7063, 16 280;
33 682, 57 712, 42 147
D 34 168, 19 449, 44 319;   21 203, 11 232,
29 466
E 1 17 234   **2** 41 616

Page 8 Division
A 9, 9, 12, 7, 2;   6, 10, 6, 5, 8;
3, 12, 0, 8, 4;   6, 11, 5, 5, 11;
11, 6, 4, 8, 9;   10, 4, 3, 12, 0;
7, 7, 10, 8, 0;   12, 10, 11, 4, 12;
9, 5, 0, 9, 0;   7, 4, 10, 11, 12
B 126, 238 r 1, 121, 103, 203 r 2;
145, 116, 473 r 1, 54 r 1, 205 r 3
C 909, 816, 400 r 2, 243 r 3, 744 r 2;
720 r 4, 709 r 1 , 621, 404, 550 r 3
D 1 1065   **2** 490   **3** 5   **4** 54   **5** 1630
6 1601   **7** 201

Page 9 Division
A 3, 8, 9, 11, 0;   3, 0, 10, 10, 6;
7, 12, 0, 4, 12;   6, 11, 5, 5, 12;
8, 9, 4, 3, 11;   10, 9, 7, 4, 6;
7, 12, 0, 2, 5;   4, 2, 6, 5, 9;
11, 3, 10, 0, 5;   6, 3, 2, 10, 4
B 135, 124, 107 r 2, 85 r 2, 80;
63 r 2, 130, 102, 59, 77 r 2
C 207 r 1, 403, 520 r 7, 931 r 4, 525 r 1;
299, 353, 400 r 3, 625 r 3, 361 r 1
D 426, 395, 506, 529, 245;
6677, 1414, 2640, 1991, 6544
E 624 r 3, 696 r 7, 892 r 7, 360 r 1;
545 r 7, 631 r 2, 693 r 5, 583 r 4
F 320, 436, 317 r 4;   540, 529, 607

Page 10 Averages
A 26, 119, 50, 28
B 1 143 cm   **2** 2   **3** 3   **4** 19 cm, 5 cm,
19 cm, 7 cm, 2 cm
C 1 17, 14, 19, 16   **2** Anni   **3** Jess   **4** Jade
D 1 320 kg   **2** 40 kg   **3** 3   **4** 4   **5** Henry
6 41 kg   **7** 45 kg   **8** 40 kg

Page 11 Long multiplication
A 1 four tens, two hundreds, nine tens,
three thousands, six ones, eight
thousands;   five ones, eight hundreds,
five thousands, six tens, four hundreds,
five tens;   seven tens, three thousands,
six ones, nine tens, eight hundreds,
five thousands
2 four hundreds, two thousands, nine
hundreds, three ten-thousands, six tens,
eight ten-thousands;   five tens, eight
thousands, five ten-thousands, six
hundreds, four thousands, five hundreds;
seven hundreds, three ten-thousands,
six tens, nine hundreds, eight thousands,
five ten-thousands
B 360, 470, 540, 700, 820, 590;
900, 1260, 1580, 1840, 500, 360;
1170, 2430, 1110, 1860, 2250, 1290;
2120, 1880, 1160, 2760, 2160, 2920
C 1050, 4680, 3150, 1710, 6720, 4560;
5520, 3360, 1850, 1440, 2030, 4860

Page 12 Long multiplication
A 432, 574, 767, 1394, 1110;
1462, 1674, 1184, 1311, 247
B 527, 7826, 1134, 5832, 2665;
693, 3162, 3408, 1148, 5734
C 2322, 2183, 1032, 3392, 4824;
1504, 3483, 3796, 3564, 6545
D 2940, 16 520, 16 760, 15 720, 26 550;
53 920, 72 090, 10 350, 10 620, 36 000
E 50 400, 40 770, 13 764, 61 503, 32 384;
27 789, 6003, 46 842, 11 856, 28 665

Page 13 Long division
A 3, 2, 2, 2, 4, 3;   2, 5, 3, 3, 2, 4
B 3 r 13, 2 r 12, 4 r 5, 3 r 6, 2 r 5, 2 r 5;
3 r 6, 2 r 14, 5 r 4, 2 r 8, 3 r 5, 4 r 5
C 7, 9, 6, 5, 8;   9, 7, 6, 8, 6
D 8 r 7, 6 r 11, 5 r 20, 9 r 11, 7 r 9;
9 r 8, 8 r 12, 7 r 14, 6 r 17, 8 r 7
E 5, 4, 5, 6, 5;   4, 5, 4, 6, 6
F 3 r 5, 4 r 5, 4 r 7, 4 r 11, 4 r 12;
6 r 1, 4 r 5, 2 r 7, 6 r 2, 6 r 8
G 7, 8, 9, 5, 9;   7, 9, 6, 6, 7
H 6 r 7, 8 r 10, 5 r 9, 8 r 8, 9 r 3

Page 14 Long division
A 12, 11, 11, 11, 14;   13, 13, 12, 12, 12
B 31, 52, 22, 32, 23;   38, 43, 47, 23, 21
C 40 r 16, 30 r 15, 20 r 9, 10 r 22, 30 r 8;
20 r 22, 40 r 11, 20 r 12, 20 r 20, 10 r 39
D 32 r 2, 52 r 7, 42 r 10, 33 r 14, 63 r 1;
31 r 15, 54 r 2, 32 r 2, 42 r 5, 21 r 10
E 72 r 6, 83, 30 r 22, 91, 82 r 20;
87 r 11, 70 r 23, 63, 43 r 6, 87
F 214, 332 r 7, 451 r 5, 416, 321;
411 r 1, 612 r 1, 291, 172 r 6, 213
G 205, 230 r 3, 106, 200 r 16, 340;
403, 600 r 13, 502 r 2, 410, 300
H 42 r 21, 363 r 2, 36 r 17, 205 r 6, 243 r 24;
34 r 1, 30 r 22, 225, 509 r 7, 410 r 16

Page 15 Problems – Long multiplication and division
1 368   **2** 21   **3a** 25   **b** 0   **4** £3.15   **5** 3350
6a 9   **b** 12   **c** 14   **7a** 5184   **b** 4032
c 6480   **8** 36   **9** £71   **10** 6480   **11a** £3.24
b £42.12 **c** £81   **12** 29 106

Page 16 Money notation
A Four pounds and seventy-two pence,
Three pounds and six pence,
Sixty-nine pence,Twenty four pounds and
twenty-two pence, Forty-one pounds,
Forty-five pence

B 1 £2.14, £4.06, £2.59;   £6.06, £4.72,
£2.05;   £3.02, £1.67, £3.21
2 324p, 521p, 1105p;   618p, 417p, 517p;
1904p, 23p, 73p
3 1, 2, 5;   2, 7, 2;   5, 0, 4;   7, 1, 2;
4, 1, 8
C 7p, £10, 40p, £200, 2p;
£10, £20, £2, £600, 70p
D 1 £55.00, £5.55, 550p, £5.05, 55p, £0.54
2 £115, 115p, £1.10, £0.15, 11p, £0.01
3 303p, £3.02, £3.00, £0.35, 34p, £0.03
4 £6.66, £6.60, 606p, 66p, £0.65, £0.06
5 213p, £2.12, £2.03, £2.02, 23p, £0.22

Page 17 Money notation
A 1 A £3.18 B £3.60 C £8.22 D £8.58
E £7.25 F £5.30   **2** £36.13
B £26.50, £4.32, £3.41, £15.00, £31.70;
£3.60, £2.82, £51.60, £4.65, £17.20
C £0.37 = 1 x 20p, 1 x 10p, 5p, 2p
£4.26 = 2 x £2, 20p, 5p, 1p
£7.18 = £5, £2, 10p, 5p, 2p, 1p
£0.78 = 50p, 20p, 5p, 2p, 1p
£11.06 = £10, £1, 5p, 1p;
£7.22 = £5, £2, 20p, 2p
£5.73 = £5, 50p, 20p, 2p, 1p
£2.14 = £2, 10p, 2 x 2p
£22.96 = £20, £2, 50p, 2 x 20p, 5p, 1p
£12.86 = £10, £2, 50p, 20p, 10p, 5p, 1p
D £1.50   **a** 150 x 1p   **b** 75 x 2p   **c** 30 x 5p
d 15 x 10p
£3.40   **a** 340 x 1p   **b** 170 x 2p   **c** 68 x 5p
d 34 x 10p
£9.70   **a** 970 x 1p   **b** 485 x 2p   **c** 194 x 5p
d 97 x 10p
£4.30   **a** 430 x 1p   **b** 215 x 2p   **c** 86 x 5p
d 43 x 10p
£8.10   **a** 810 x 1p   **b** 405 x 2p   **c** 162 x 5p
d 81 x 10p

Page 18 Money – addition and subtraction
A £6.66, £48.60;   £22.19, £74.53;
£32.14, £34.65;   £26.33, £56.74;   £12.33,
£93.13;   £36.18, £46.98;   £30.04, £12.54;
£55.19, £17.13;   £66.53, £29.39;   £13.77,
£27.00
B £2.81, £9.03;   £3.65, £1.05;   £3.29,
£2.63;   £2.82, £13.92;   £9.01, £27.96;
£8.31, £18.99;   £2.67, £4.67;   £7.08, £10.80;
£1.89, £3.60;   £0.56, £11.76
C £36.37;   £18.57

Page 19 Money – multiplication and division
A £16.68, £50.80, £193.04, £116.90;
£7.68, £36.78, £194.16, £116.68;
£109.53, £160.75, £113.44, £82.24;
£192.48, £97.74, £4.95, £65.44;
£68.25, £108.85, £219.44, £96.39
B £1.14, £2.32, £7.37, £3.83;   £3.14, £4.02,
£4.57, £0.13;   £31.62, £3.93, £6.04, £4.88;
£4.72, £2.74, £22.42, £21.73;
£1.20, £18.27, £35.44, £16.18
C £2.12, £1.26, £2.71;   £1.73, £3.48, £4.05

Page 20 Money problems
1 £22.72   **2** £3.11   **3** £24.75   **4** £7.25
5 £0.85   **6** £2.40   **7** £39.10   **8** £1.46
9 £3.53   **10** £2.75   **11a** £8.20   **b** 30p
12 £7.84

Page 21 Bills
1 36p, 54p, 37p, 28p = £1.55   **2** 72p, £1.44,
18p, £3.00 = £5.34   **3** £1.96, £1.26, £1.08,
£1.38 = £5.68   **4** £7.32, £47.37, £2.52,
£19.50, £8.25 = £84.96   **5** £1.14, £3.15,
£3.85, £2.22 = £10.36   **6** £1.18, £0.84, £0.72,
£3.88 = £6.62

Page 22 Fractions
1a $\frac{5}{12}$ **b** $\frac{7}{12}$ **2a** $\frac{4}{9}$ **b** $\frac{5}{9}$ **3a** $\frac{7}{8}$ **b** $\frac{1}{8}$

4a $\frac{1}{2}$ **b** $\frac{1}{2}$ **5a** $\frac{3}{4}$ **b** $\frac{1}{4}$ **6a** $\frac{2}{5}$ **b** $\frac{3}{5}$

7a $\frac{11}{20}$ **b** $\frac{9}{20}$ **8a** $\frac{3}{7}$ **b** $\frac{4}{7}$ **9a** $\frac{7}{10}$ **b** $\frac{3}{10}$

10a $\frac{1}{6}$ **b** $\frac{5}{6}$ **11a** $\frac{1}{3}$ **b** $\frac{2}{3}$ **12a** $\frac{5}{16}$ **b** $\frac{11}{16}$

Page 23 Fractions
18, 8, 3, 8;   6, 10, 20, 16;   2, 5, 5, 16;
3, 2, 2, 2;   6, 8, 4, 16;   14, 12, 16, 1;
8, 4, 2, 3;   5, 3, 16, 12;   2, 10, 3, 10;
15, 3, 5, 20

Page 24 Fractions
A 8, 24, 15
B $\frac{8}{10} > \frac{7}{10}$, $\frac{5}{6} > \frac{4}{6}$, $\frac{15}{20} = \frac{15}{20}$, $\frac{9}{12} > \frac{8}{12}$, $\frac{13}{20} < \frac{14}{20}$;
$\frac{9}{12} < \frac{10}{12}$, $\frac{8}{12} < \frac{9}{12}$, $\frac{5}{10} > \frac{4}{10}$, $\frac{6}{8} > \frac{5}{8}$, $\frac{17}{20} > \frac{16}{20}$
C $\frac{4}{5}$, $\frac{1}{3}$, $\frac{3}{4}$, $\frac{2}{3}$, $\frac{3}{4}$, $\frac{1}{2}$, $\frac{3}{4}$, $\frac{7}{10}$, $\frac{4}{5}$, $\frac{5}{6}$
D $\frac{7}{2}$, $\frac{29}{4}$, $\frac{8}{5}$, $\frac{14}{3}$, $\frac{61}{10}$, $\frac{19}{8}$, $\frac{23}{6}$, $\frac{23}{20}$, $\frac{32}{15}$, $\frac{32}{9}$
E $3\frac{3}{4}$, $1\frac{3}{10}$, $2\frac{5}{8}$, $2\frac{5}{6}$, $1\frac{3}{20}$, $6\frac{1}{2}$, $5\frac{4}{5}$,
$5\frac{5}{6}$, $1\frac{7}{12}$, $2\frac{4}{9}$
F $1\frac{3}{5}$, $4\frac{1}{2}$, $4\frac{1}{2}$, $1\frac{1}{5}$, $1\frac{1}{3}$, $1\frac{2}{3}$, $4\frac{1}{2}$, $1\frac{3}{7}$, $1\frac{1}{6}$, $5\frac{1}{3}$

Page 25 Addition of fractions

A $\frac{4}{5}, \frac{4}{5}, \frac{4}{5}, \frac{5}{6}$; $\frac{1}{2}, \frac{3}{4}, \frac{14}{15}, \frac{2}{3}$

B $1\frac{1}{5}$; $1\frac{1}{2}, 1\frac{1}{2}, 1\frac{2}{3}$; $1\frac{2}{5}, 1\frac{3}{5}, 1\frac{5}{8}, 1\frac{5}{7}$

C $\frac{7}{10}, \frac{3}{4}, \frac{7}{8}, \frac{19}{20}$; $\frac{13}{16}, \frac{3}{4}, \frac{7}{8}, \frac{7}{9}$

D $1\frac{1}{2}$; $1\frac{1}{6}, 1\frac{1}{20}, 1\frac{3}{4}$; $1\frac{9}{14}, 1\frac{4}{15}, 1\frac{3}{8}, 1\frac{5}{8}$

E $\frac{13}{24}, \frac{11}{12}, \frac{9}{10}, \frac{17}{18}$; $\frac{13}{18}, \frac{19}{24}, \frac{17}{24}, \frac{17}{20}$

F $1\frac{13}{24}, 1\frac{5}{18}, 1\frac{3}{20}, 1\frac{7}{24}$;
$1\frac{17}{24}, 1\frac{5}{24}, 1\frac{23}{60}, 1\frac{13}{18}$

G $3\frac{1}{2}, 5\frac{9}{10}, 4\frac{13}{14}, 5\frac{19}{24}$;
$2\frac{19}{20}, 5\frac{11}{16}, 5\frac{17}{30}, 4\frac{19}{20}$

H $6\frac{13}{30}, 6\frac{9}{14}, 8\frac{11}{20}, 10\frac{5}{12}$;
$6\frac{13}{24}, 6\frac{13}{20}, 11\frac{1}{24}, 10\frac{1}{3}$

I $1\frac{1}{12}, 1\frac{1}{6}, 1\frac{13}{60}$; $4\frac{17}{20}, 4\frac{9}{20}, 8\frac{5}{6}$

Page 26 Subtraction of fractions

A $\frac{1}{3}, \frac{2}{5}, \frac{1}{5}, \frac{3}{10}$; $\frac{4}{15}, \frac{4}{15}, \frac{1}{2}, \frac{1}{4}$

B $\frac{3}{10}, \frac{1}{6}, \frac{3}{20}, \frac{1}{4}$; $\frac{5}{16}, \frac{3}{14}, \frac{1}{3}, \frac{3}{20}$

C $\frac{7}{12}, \frac{1}{20}, \frac{5}{18}, \frac{7}{24}$; $\frac{1}{24}, \frac{7}{30}, \frac{1}{6}, \frac{3}{20}$

D $\frac{1}{4}, \frac{1}{8}, \frac{1}{6}, \frac{1}{12}$; $2\frac{1}{16}, 4\frac{1}{20}, 6\frac{2}{15}, 3\frac{1}{14}$

E $1\frac{3}{8}, 3\frac{7}{20}, 1\frac{1}{4}, 6\frac{1}{4}$; $1\frac{7}{30}, 3\frac{3}{16}, 2\frac{2}{15}, 7\frac{1}{16}$

F $1\frac{3}{8}, 3\frac{1}{10}, 1\frac{13}{20}, 1\frac{1}{20}$; $5\frac{1}{3}, 2\frac{1}{12}, 2\frac{19}{30}, 3\frac{2}{9}$

G $2\frac{1}{4}, 2\frac{1}{8}, \frac{1}{12}, 2\frac{3}{10}$; $\frac{11}{20}, 4\frac{1}{16}, 2\frac{1}{9}, 1\frac{2}{15}$

H $\frac{4}{5}, 1\frac{11}{12}, 3\frac{9}{16}, \frac{17}{20}$; $2\frac{13}{30}, 5\frac{5}{8}, 6\frac{13}{20}, 1\frac{11}{12}$

I $3\frac{3}{10}, 4\frac{1}{6}, 6\frac{7}{12}, 1\frac{1}{10}$; $6\frac{7}{9}, 1\frac{5}{12}, 1\frac{5}{6}, 1\frac{13}{16}$

Page 27 Multiplication of fractions

A $\frac{3}{4}, \frac{2}{3}, \frac{3}{5}, \frac{3}{4}, \frac{7}{12}, \frac{1}{2}, \frac{4}{5}, \frac{4}{5}, \frac{4}{5}, \frac{3}{4}$. $\frac{3}{4}, \frac{1}{2}, \frac{2}{3}, \frac{4}{5}$,
$\frac{8}{9}, \frac{1}{4}, \frac{2}{3}, \frac{4}{5}, \frac{2}{3}, \frac{7}{8}$

B $\frac{15}{16}, \frac{8}{9}, \frac{5}{6}, \frac{9}{20}$; $\frac{10}{11}, \frac{15}{16}, \frac{4}{5}, \frac{7}{12}$

C $3\frac{3}{5}, 2\frac{1}{2}, 3\frac{1}{2}, 2\frac{2}{5}$; $2\frac{1}{4}, 1\frac{1}{4}, 2\frac{2}{7}, 1\frac{1}{3}$

D $\frac{1}{5}, \frac{4}{7}, \frac{8}{15}, \frac{11}{21}$; $\frac{3}{4}, \frac{3}{4}, \frac{1}{4}, \frac{4}{33}$

E $1\frac{3}{5}, 2\frac{2}{3}, 2\frac{1}{16}, 2$; $1\frac{1}{2}, 1\frac{1}{5}, 2, 1\frac{1}{3}$

F $8\frac{3}{4}, 19\frac{1}{4}, 3\frac{2}{3}, 15$; $8, 7\frac{3}{16}, 13\frac{1}{2}, 18$

G $24, 3\frac{1}{2}, 5\frac{7}{10}, 3\frac{1}{3}$; $1, 3\frac{1}{3}, 9, 10$

Page 28 Division of fractions

A $\frac{2}{5}, \frac{3}{10}, \frac{3}{7}, \frac{3}{16}$; $\frac{3}{16}, \frac{3}{11}, \frac{1}{9}, \frac{4}{25}$

B $\frac{1}{5}, \frac{2}{7}, 1\frac{2}{5}, \frac{3}{4}$; $\frac{2}{3}, 2\frac{1}{2}, \frac{2}{9}, \frac{3}{4}$

C 12, 42, 60, 24; 20, 10, $12\frac{4}{5}$, 10

D 5, $3\frac{1}{3}, 2\frac{2}{3}, 7\frac{1}{5}$; $1\frac{1}{2}, 1\frac{1}{5}, 3\frac{1}{3}, 1\frac{1}{3}$

E $1\frac{5}{7}, 1\frac{3}{11}, 1\frac{1}{10}, 1\frac{1}{3}$; $\frac{3}{4}, \frac{4}{5}, \frac{3}{5}, 3\frac{6}{7}$

F $\frac{5}{6}, \frac{2}{9}, \frac{1}{2}, \frac{1}{3}$; $\frac{6}{35}, \frac{11}{40}, \frac{1}{4}, \frac{1}{6}$

G $5\frac{1}{2}, 5\frac{5}{6}, 2\frac{2}{3}, 18$; $1\frac{2}{3}, 4, 3, 2\frac{1}{2}$

H $\frac{2}{3}, 1\frac{3}{5}, 2\frac{2}{15}, 1\frac{1}{4}$; $\frac{2}{3}, 1\frac{1}{9}, 6, 2\frac{2}{3}$; $\frac{8}{9}, \frac{27}{32}, \frac{16}{21}, 1\frac{7}{8}$

Page 29 Fractional parts

A 48p, 75 g, 49, 45 m; £2.00, 220, 510, 100 km; 180 g, 84, 27p, 20 kg; 60p, 54, 258, £570; 110 cm, 700, £1.95, 120 km; £42.00, 45 g, 248 g, 350 g; 900, 115 km, 150 m, £2.70

B £1.50, 120 g, 245 m, 120 l; 60p, 105, £49.00, 180 km; £15.00, 1000 g, 200, £1.50; 600 m, £4.95, 120 kg , 96

C $\frac{1}{2}$, $\frac{3}{4}$, $\frac{3}{4}$, $\frac{1}{2}$

Page 30 Decimal notation

A 1 0·07, 0·9, 0·1, 0·15, 0·13, 0·04, 0·3, 0·6, 0·63, 0·11; **2** 0·19, 0·06; 0·2, 0·21, 0·02, 0·8 **3** 1·8, 1·41; 2·5, 1·08; 14·6, 2·29
4 4·07, 3·9, 6·14, 8·7, 9·03, 11·43, 12·63, 4·1

B four tenths, eight ones, seven hundredths, one hundred, four thousands;
two hundredths, six ones, four hundreds, four tenths, eight tens

C 1 426, 326, 25, 112·7, 460; 352·6, 3245, 0·1, 206, 4510 **2** 4·27, 1·36, 1·12, 14·32, 1·46; 0·02, 0·02, 14·71, 0·66, 2·43

D 1 21, 30, 7, 143, 49, 160, 3, 124
2 23, 406, 230, 7, 427, 326, 9, 11

Page 31 Decimal notation

A 1 0·004, 0·016, 0·216, 0·019, 0·002, 0·303, 0·043, 0·021 **2** 0·025, 0·101; 0·014, 0·008; 0·016, 0·250

B 7, 16, 120, 436, 820, 9; 125, 27, 360, 207, 5, 750

C 43·00, 40·03, 4·3, 4·003, 0·43, 0·043; 11·2, 11·02, 11·002, 1·12, 1·102, 1·012; 91·0, 90·01, 9·01, 0·91, 0·901, 0·091

D 1 2400, 261, 5000, 4010, 3006, 6270, 3415, 2600 **2** 4·231, 0·041, 0·321, 0·006, 0·012, 3·421, 0·018, 0·106

E a ×10 **b** ×1000 **c** ×10 000 **d** nothing (or ×1) **e** ÷10 **f** ×100 000 **g** ×100

F 1 4200, 34·5, 410, 1·1, 1·0
2 2·641, 0·026, 0·006, 0·027, 0·001

Page 32 Decimals – addition and subtraction

A 18·045, 51·318;   240·85, 93·845;
347·257, 1325·32;   27·331, 1768·644;
35·645, 463·878

B 231·828, 15·385;   81·383, 235·463;
88·381, 126·247;   148·732, 25·046;
120·045, 28·253

C 0·99, 0·352;   0·891, 1·05;   0·074, 0·094;
0·377, 0·054;   1·384, 102·559

D 7·11, 1·041;   122·892, 59·055;
67·93, 208·938;   5·066, 193·713

Page 33 Decimals – multiplication and division

A 1 0·28, 1·8, 4·00, 0·015;
4·2, 0·015, 2·8, 0·81; 0·034, 0·64
2 0·84, 0·117, 1·20, 2·73;
0·200, 2·24, 2·46, 0·198
3 12·0, 33·6, 20·8, 46·2, 28·8, 52·0;
6·28, 20·40, 60·48, 64·72, 55·44, 22·89
4 3·435, 10·355, 48·264, 82·881, 28·063;
10·210, 32·524, 43·254, 6·705, 7·856
B 1 0·8, 0·6, 0·9; 0·06, 0·08, 0·11;
0·8, 0·8;   0·12, 0·07
2 0·14, 0·13, 0·02, 0·19, 0·48
3 0·15, 0·32, 0·84, 0·52, 0·94
4 3·56, 1·43, 3·25, 4·56, 3·11;
5·42, 6·49, 4·23, 4·54, 9·87
5 0·142, 0·813, 0·522, 0·797, 0·628;
0·615, 1·674, 1·687, 1·642, 1·576

Page 34 Approximations

A 1 150, 270, 470, 740, 620, 550, 340, 840
2 3400, 6400, 7800, 11 800, 3000, 1700;
15 000, 4800, 9700, 9300, 12 400, 8500
3 14 000, 33 000, 27 000, 20 000, 8000;
31 000, 55 000, 62 000, 82 000, 73 000
4 43·2, 124·6, 9·2, 88·8, 63·0;
47·4, 125·6, 22·7, 90·5, 90·0
5 19, 45, 34, 103, 22, 45;
12, 82, 132, 90, 129, 56
6 33·36, 82·17, 15·18, 81·14, 68·35;
66·22, 44·16, 222·38, 54·28, 77·28
B 1a 15 474   **b** 15 470   **c** 15 500   **d** 15 000
2a 23 628   **b** 23 630   **c** 23 600   **d** 24 000
3a 88 459   **b** 88 460   **c** 88 500   **d** 88 000
4a 102 654   **b** 102 650   **c** 102 700
d 103 000
5a 18 753   **b** 18 750   **c** 18 800   **d** 19 000
6a 32 817   **b** 32 820   **c** 32 800   **d** 33 000

7a 21 433   **b** 21 430   **c** 21 400   **d** 21 000
8a 73 000   **b** 73 000   **c** 73 000   **d** 73 000

Page 35 Percentages

A 2a 24%   **b** 76%   **3a** 47%   **b** 53%
4a 64%   **b** 36%   **5a** 85%   **b** 15%
6a 54%   **b** 46%   **7a** 32%   **b** 68%
8a 31% **b** 69%   **9a** 40%   **b** 60%   **10a** 64%
b 36%
B a 9%   **b** 14%   **c** 12%   **d** 2%   **e** 4%
b 59%
C Anni   **a** $\frac{47}{100}$ **b** 47%   **a** $\frac{98}{100}$ **b** 98%
a $\frac{86}{100}$ **b** 86%
Connor   **a** $\frac{49}{100}$ **b** 49%   **a** $\frac{47}{100}$ **b** 47%
a $\frac{99}{100}$ **b** 99%
Jake   **a** $\frac{73}{100}$ **b** 73%   **a** $\frac{82}{100}$ **b** 82%
a $\frac{75}{100}$ **b** 75%
Jess   **a** $\frac{86}{100}$ **b** 86%   **a** $\frac{78}{100}$ **b** 78%
a $\frac{44}{100}$ **b** 44%
Emily   **a** $\frac{94}{100}$ **b** 94%   **a** $\frac{91}{100}$ **b** 91%
a $\frac{96}{100}$ **b** 96%
Mo   **a** $\frac{35}{100}$ **b** 35%   **a** $\frac{74}{100}$ **b** 74%
a $\frac{82}{100}$ **b** 82%
Naz   **a** $\frac{90}{100}$ **b** 90%   **a** $\frac{67}{100}$ **b** 67%
a $\frac{84}{100}$ **b** 84%
Paul   **a** $\frac{81}{100}$ **b** 81%   **a** $\frac{97}{100}$ **b** 97%
a $\frac{41}{100}$ **b** 41%
Mark   **a** $\frac{74}{100}$ **b** 74%   **a** $\frac{98}{100}$ **b** 98%
a $\frac{97}{100}$ **b** 97%
Chloe   **a** $\frac{66}{100}$ **b** 66%   **a** $\frac{88}{100}$ **b** 88%
a $\frac{96}{100}$ **b** 96%

Page 36 Percentages

A 25, $\frac{25}{100}$, 0·25, 25%;   20, $\frac{20}{100}$, 0·20, 20%;
$12\frac{1}{2}$, $\frac{12\frac{1}{2}}{100}$, 0·125, $12\frac{1}{2}$%;   10, $\frac{10}{100}$, 0·10
10%;   5, $\frac{5}{100}$, 0·05, 5%;
4, $\frac{4}{100}$, 0·04, 4%;   2, $\frac{2}{100}$, 0·02, 2%
B 75%, 80%, 30%, 28%, 34%, 44%, 65%,
$87\frac{1}{2}$ %, 60%, $62\frac{1}{2}$%, 22%, 35%;   98%,
76%, 40%, 45%, 86%, 12%, 96%, 66%,
95%, 46%, 70%, 90%
C $\frac{1}{4}$, $\frac{18}{25}$, $\frac{3}{10}$, $\frac{3}{5}$, $\frac{3}{4}$, $\frac{29}{100}$, $\frac{22}{25}$, $\frac{9}{10}$, $\frac{4}{25}$, $\frac{7}{20}$; $\frac{9}{50}$, $\frac{33}{50}$,
$\frac{13}{100}$, $\frac{17}{20}$, $\frac{31}{50}$, $\frac{9}{20}$, $\frac{4}{5}$, $\frac{7}{10}$, $\frac{19}{25}$, $\frac{8}{25}$
D 1 F $\frac{1}{2}$, R $\frac{1}{4}$, C $\frac{1}{8}$, T $\frac{1}{8}$ **2** F 50%, R 25%,
C $12\frac{1}{2}$ %, T $12\frac{1}{2}$%   **3a** 20   **b** 10   **c** 5   **d** 5
E 1 84%, 90%, 75%, 85%, 50%   **2** F 4,

H 1, F 4, M 3, E 6 **3** F 16%, H 10%, F 25%, M 15%, E 50%

Page 37 Percentages

A 1 20%, 7%, 25%, 36%, 27%, 32%, 72%, 85% **2** 35%, $22\frac{1}{2}$%, 74%, 63%, 2%, 6%
3 20%, 40%, 70%, 4%, 5%, 25%, 75%
B 1a $\frac{35}{50}$ **b** 70%, **a** $\frac{20}{200}$ **b** 10%,
a $\frac{56}{100}$ **b** 56%, **a** $\frac{15}{20}$, **b** 75%;
a $\frac{25}{250}$ **b** 10%, **a** $\frac{36}{50}$ **b** 72%,
a $\frac{9}{36}$ **b** 25%, **a** $\frac{15}{60}$ **b** 25%;
a $\frac{21}{105}$ **b** 20%, **a** $\frac{90}{250}$ **b** 36%,
a $\frac{32}{50}$ **b** 64%, **a** $\frac{12}{25}$ **b** 48%
2 5p, 15p, 35p, 36p, 47p;
25p, £1.15, £1.70, £2.40, £2.55;
8p, £1.28, £1.92, £2.40, £3.60
C 7p, $2\frac{1}{2}$ m, 3p; 18, 9 g, 99;
50 kg, 45, 1·5 mm; 12p, 50, 60

D a 8 kg, 24 kg, 56 kg, 72 kg **b** 70 m, 140 m, 210 m, 280 m **c** 10 g, 30 g, 50 g, 70 g **d** 13 l, 26 l, 39 l, 52 l

Page 38 Capacity – notation

A 1 275 ml, 3629 ml, 2530 ml, 5036 ml, 52 ml; 4326 ml, 7 ml, 8040 ml, 6271 ml, 10 130 ml
2 3·269 l, 0·629 l, 2·014 l, 16·141 l, 2·13 l; 14·321 l, 0·076 l, 0·127 l, 0·52 l, 0·026 l
3 2·2 l, 2200 ml; 3·75 l, 3750 ml; 0·9 l, 900 ml; 4·5 l, 4500 ml; 6·8 l, 6800 ml; 2·25 l, 2250 ml; 5·3 l, 5300 ml; 1·6 l, 1600 ml
4 175 ml, 8 ml, 346 ml, 239 ml, 304 ml, 79 ml
5 93 ml, 211 ml, 13 ml, 142 ml, 243 ml, 31 ml
B 1 3000 ml **2** 100 ml
3 and **4**

	A	B	C	D	E	F	G	H	I	J	K	L
ml	2400	1700	2800	2200	900	400	200	1400	1100	2500	1900	600
a l	2·4	1·7	2·8	2·2	0·9	0·4	0·2	1·4	1·1	2·5	1·9	0·6
b l	$2\frac{2}{5}$	$1\frac{7}{10}$	$2\frac{4}{5}$	$2\frac{1}{5}$	$\frac{9}{10}$	$\frac{2}{5}$	$\frac{1}{5}$	$1\frac{2}{5}$	$1\frac{1}{10}$	$2\frac{1}{2}$	$1\frac{9}{10}$	$\frac{3}{5}$

5 1 l 200 ml or 1·2 l or 1200 ml
6 a 0·3 l **b** 0·8 l **c** 1·3 l **d** 1·8 l

Page 39 Capacity – addition and subtraction

A 1 1·2 l < 1241 ml, 3·400 l = $3\frac{2}{5}$ l, 807 ml > 0·087 l; $\frac{3}{4}$ l < 752 ml, 2·150 l > 2050 ml, 8·070 l > 870 ml; 0·6 l > 575 ml, 50 ml = 0·050 l, $\frac{3}{4}$ l > 0·600 l; 0·9 l > 892 ml, 800 ml = $\frac{4}{5}$ l, 3·261 l < 3621 ml
2 2 l, 4 l, 5 l, 8 l, 4 l; 4 l, 17 l, 1 l, 4 l, 7 l
3 $2\frac{1}{2}$ l, 2 l, $\frac{1}{2}$ l, 3 l, $4\frac{1}{2}$ l; $3\frac{1}{2}$ l, $4\frac{1}{2}$ l, 8 l, 6 l, $61\frac{1}{2}$ l
B 1

	230 ml	650 ml	380 ml	191 ml	320 ml	962 ml	55 ml	332 ml	754 ml	909 ml	621 ml	451 ml
a ml	770	350	620	809	680	38	945	668	246	91	379	549
b l	1·270	0·850	1·120	1·309	1·180	0·538	1·445	1·168	0·746	0·591	0·879	1·049
c l	1·770	1·350	1·620	1·809	1·680	1·038	1·945	1·668	1·246	1·091	1·379	1·549

2a nil   **b** 1 ml   **c** 724 ml   **d** 540 ml
C 1a 3·5 l   **b** 3500 ml   **2a** 7·25 l   **b** 7250 ml
3a 5·250 l   **b** 5250

Page 40 Mass
A 1·6 kg, 950 g;   1·3 kg, 1·71 kg;
1·35 kg, 1·1 kg;   850 g, 1·84 kg
B 1 0·3 kg, 0·7 kg, 0·05 kg, 0·075 kg,
0·25 kg, 0·08 kg, 0·95 kg, 0·085 kg
2 3·45 kg, 1·25 kg, 4·32 kg, 5·006 kg,
7·341 kg, 9·22 kg
C 1 250 g, 600 g, 300 g, 750 g, 400 g,
700 g, 800 g, 100 g, 200 g
2 1500 g, 3400 g, 4750 g, 6300 g, 8600 g,
7250 g, 2700 g, 4800 g
3 1620 g, 770 g, 1460 g, 1600 g, 3700 g,
700 g, 900 g
D >, >;   <, <;   <, >;   >, >;   >, <

Page 41 Mass
A 1 3 t 216 kg, 2 t 141 kg, 6 t 20 kg,
8 t 25 kg, 1 t 416 kg, 3 t 219 kg
2 4·126 t, 0·347 t, 0·074 t, 0·092 t, 1·146 t,
0·096 t, 0·175 t
3 236 kg, 14 kg, 6016 kg, 236 kg, 8212 kg,
17 kg
4 3·944 t, 2·686 t;   1·761 t, 6·989 t;
95·122 t, 4·060 t;   8·840 t, 4·668 t
B 1 5 kg   **2a** 0·3 kg   **b** 0·7 kg   **b** 1·3 kg
d 1·7 kg   **e** 2·2 kg   **f** 2·5 kg   **g** 2·7 kg
h 3·2 kg   **i** 3·5 kg   **j** 3·7 kg   **k** 4·3 kg
l 4·6 kg
C 1 1 kg   **2** 10 g   **3 q** 60 g **r** 150 g **s** 230 g
t 350 g **u** 500 g **v** 570 g **w** 710 g
x 850 g **y** 900 g **z** 970 g

Page 42 Length
A 1 3026 mm, 15 400 mm, 6075 mm,
3750 mm, 26 mm
2 3·241 m, 8·186 m, 0·074 m, 0·009 m,
0·147 m;   0·525 m, 0·064 m, 4·025 m,
0·006 m, 4·396 m
3 3500 m, 4200 m, 7250 m, 6750 m,
375 m; 6750 m, 3300 m, 4800 m,
1070 m; 3750 m
4 3250 m   **a** 3 km 250 m   **b** 3·250 km;
1742 m   **a** 1 km 742 m   **b** 1·742 km;
1035 m   **a** 1 km 35 m   **b** 1·035 km;
2072 m   **a** 2 km 72 m   **b** 2·072 km;

3153 m   **a** 3 km 153 m   **b** 3·153 km;
4320 m   **a** 4 km 320 m   **b** 4·320 km;
2065 m   **a** 2 km 65 m   **b** 2·065 km;
4635 m   **a** 4 km 635 m   **b** 4·635 km;
4340 m   **a** 4 km 340 m   **b** 4·34 km;
1007 m   **a** 1 km 7 m   **b** 1·007 km
B 1 33 cm, 7 cm, 3 cm, 81 cm
2 22 m, 16 m, 29 m, 51 m, 43 m;
1 m, 4 m, 6 m, 7 m, 4 m
3 5 km, 7 km, 2 km, 8 km, 9 km;
43 km, 63 km, 126 km, 26 km, 6 km
4 147 cm, 630 cm, 1243 cm, 73 cm, 68 cm

Page 43 Length
A 1 A 96 mm, B 136 mm, C 40 mm,
D 100 mm, E 115 mm, F 56 mm
2 19 mm, 60 mm;   21 mm, 40 mm,
96 mm, 40 mm;   44 mm, 75 mm
3a C and F   **b** A and C
4 D + F, A + C + F   **5** 61 mm, 52 mm
B 1a 24 mm   **b** 18 mm   **c** 84 mm
2a 45 mm   **b** 23 mm   **c** 136 mm
3a 66 mm   **b** 8 mm   **c** 148 mm
4a 31 mm   **b** 31 mm   **c** 124 mm
5a 49 mm   **b** 26 mm   **c** 150 mm
6a 53 mm   **b** 35 mm   **c** 176 mm

Page 44 Area and perimeter
A a 22 cm   **b** 23 cm^2 **B a** 18 cm   **b** 8 cm^2
C a 30 cm   **b** 24 cm^2 **D a** 26 cm
b 15 cm^2 **E a** 20 cm   **b** 9 cm^2 **F a** 16 cm
b 9 cm^2 **G a** 22 cm   **b** 10 cm^2
H a 40 cm   **b** 34 cm^2

Page 45 Scale drawing
A 1 40, 60, 87·5, 85·0, 92·5, 55·0, 120, 62·5,
100, 72·5, 52·5, 97·5
2 4, 15, 25, 6, 9, 3, 20, 2, 13, 17, 10, 7
3 scale lengths $4\frac{3}{4}$, 13, 12, 4, $5\frac{3}{4}$, $12\frac{1}{2}$
true lengths 18, 26, 12, 13, 38, 40
B 1 A – B 8 m, B – C 5 m, C – D 8 m,
D – A 5 m
2 A – B 50 m, B – C 30 m, C – D 15 m,
D – E 10 m, E – F 35 m, F – A 20 m
3 A – B 2 m, B – C 0·75 m, C – D 1·5 m,
D – A 1·25 m
4 A – B 37·5 km, B – C 10 km, C – D 20 km,
D – A 12·5 km
C 850 m, 750 m, 1250 m, 1050 m, 1350 m

Page 46 Scale drawing

A a 32·5 cm   **b** 46 cm   **c** 55·5 cm
d 62 cm   **e** 25·5 cm

B 1a 2·3 cm, 4 cm, 3·8 cm, 12 cm, 18 cm, 4·8 cm
b 3·5 cm, 4·8 cm, 7·3 cm, 8·6 cm, 12 cm, 10·5 cm

C kitchen – length 10 m, width 10 m, area 100 m²
hall – length 10 m, width 4 m, area 40 m²
sitting room – length 12 m, width 10 m, area 120 m²
dining room – length 10 m, width 6 m, area 60 m²

D a (i) length 5 m, width 4 m
(ii) length 1·7 m, width 0·9 m
(iii) length 1 m, width 0·3 m
(iv) length 1·5 m, width 0·6 m
b (i) 2·5 m **(ii)** 1 m

Page 47 Approximations

A 1 4 m, 15 m, 19 m, 4 m, 25 m;
16 m, 13 m, 26 m, 3 m, 16 m
2 4 km, 24 km, 34 km, 126 km, 9 km;
14 km, 14 km, 22 km, 84 km, 127 km
3 4 kg, 17 kg, 24 kg, 1 kg, 32 kg;
16 kg, 86 kg, 54 kg, 126 kg, 24 kg
4 £2.00, £41.00, £62.00, £54.00, £8.00, £9.00;   £4.00, £7.00, £26.00, £19.00, £36.00, £54.00
5 33, £7.00, 4, 47, 822, 4·0 km;
20 l, 7 km, 10, 8, 98 l, 277 m;
100, 21 cm, 46p, 6 kg, 11, 42 km
B 1 55 000, 35 000, 42 000, 35 000, 40 000, 40 000
2 Bolton v Chelsea, Southampton v Norwich
3 Arsenal v Man. City, Aston Villa v Birmingham

Page 48 Measures

1 800 sacks   **2** 1160 tubs   **3** 143 cm
4 42 cm   **5** £11.25   **6** 88 packets   **7** 120
8 40   **9** 50 kg   **10** 250 m   **11a** 22p
b £3.52   **c** £5.94   **12** 6 l

Page 49 Telling time

A 1:23, 10:12, 3:51, 10:41, 8:24;
2:41, 6:38, 8:31, 5:11, 8:59
B 15 min to 5, 26 min past 6, 28 min to 10, 5 min past 4, 12 min past 2, 4 min to 7, 15 min to 10, 21 min past 7;   7 min to 2, 16 min past 4, 29 min to 9, 11 min to 4, 23 min past 5, 13 min to 11, 18 min past 11, 19 min to 1
C 7:06, 9:49, 4:01, 10:27, 1:03, 11:16, 11:02; 4:26, 3:00, 9:19, 8:41, 2:04, 7:50, 6:05
D 6:51, 6:09, 8:59, 11:17, 10:34, 1:48, 8:00; 12:50, 2:57, 5:05, 12:41, 3:56, 6:55, 1:54
E 15 min, 28 min, 7 min, 46 min, 51 min, 37 min, 53 min;   48 min, 42 min, 18 min, 13 min, 22 min, 35 min, 41 min

Page 50 Telling time

A 1 A 2:58, 2 min to 3 B 5:20, 20 min past 5 C 6:02, 2 min past 6
D 8:29, 29 min past 8 E 11:44, 16 min to 12
2 B 2 h 22 min, C 3 h 4 min, D 5 h 31 min, E 8 h 46 min
B 7 h 20 min, 4 h 8 min;   3 h 9 min, 7 h 35 min;   4 h 28 min, 7 h 24 min; 43 min, 6 h 59 min
C 1 60 min, 30 min, 15 min, 12 min;
5 min, 10 min, 20 min, 6 min;
144 min, 125 min, 225 min, 258 min;
340 min, 470 min, 108 min, 282 min;
85 min, 216 min, 335 min, 295 min
2 83 min, 166 min, 307 min;   554 min, 196 min, 389 min;   272 min, 424 min
D 2 h 22 min, 1 h 16 min, 4 h 13 min, 1 h 31 min, 2 h 12 min, 1 h 9 min;
3 h 32 min, 1 h 23 min, 2 h 59 min, 1 h 29 min, 5 h 45 min, 2 h 44 min
E 150 seconds, 225 seconds, 495 seconds, 276 seconds, 342 seconds, 415 seconds

Page 51 Telling time

A 1 seventeen minutes to eight, twelve minutes past nine, twenty-eight minutes to twelve, one minute to eleven, twenty-four minutes to five;

twenty-nine minutes past one, seven minutes to seven, nineteen minutes to nine, seven minutes to six, thirteen minutes to one
2 0945, 0625;   0800, 0936; 0347, 1242, 1005
B 1 9:35, 9:55, 10:15, 10:35, 10:55, 11:15, 11:35, 11:55, 12:15, 12:35, 12:55, 1:15
2 8:12, 8:27, 8:42, 8:57, 9:12, 9:27, 9:42, 9:57, 10:12, 10:27, 10:42, 10:57
C BBC 1 h 15 min; 15 min; 30 min; 25 min; 25 min; 10 min; 45 min; 30 min
ITV 25 min; 25 min; 20 min; 15 min; 10 min; 55 min; 10 min; 20 min

Page 52 24 hour clock
A 1 04:15, 07:30, 06:20, 11:43, 09:16, 03:11; 10:47, 06:35, 02:36, 01:52, 05:06, 08:25
2 4:12 am, 9:32 am, 8:54 am, 12:29 pm, 7:49 am, 8:03 am; 3:51 am, 11:23 am, 5:42 am, 6:07 am, 10:38 am, 1:16 am
B 1 13:29, 16:46, 15:34, 12:05, 22:16, 17:12; 14:21, 23:45, 21:38, 20:56, 18:51, 19:09
2 2:41 pm, 4:32 pm, 11:27 pm, 1:23 pm, 10:35 pm, 7:48 pm; 8:56 pm, 6:07 pm, 3:16 pm, 9:51 pm, 5:54 pm, 4:09 pm
C 1 13:19, 07:07, 02:46, 23:25, 15:58, 10:47; 00:38, 04:55, 20:18, 06:02, 21:33, 17:20
2 7:09 am, 9 min past 7; 1:36 pm, 24 min to 2; 4:26 am, 26 min past 4; 3:19 pm, 19 min past 3; 11:46 pm, 14 min to 12; 6:54 am, 6 min to 7; 9:49 am, 11 min to 10; 2:50 am, 10 min to 3; 6:05 pm, 5 min past 6; 9:23 pm, 23 min past 9; 8:22 am, 22 min past 8; 8:13 pm, 13 min past 8

Page 53 Timetables
A journey ends 18:02, 05:13, 07:35, 16:24, 20:55, 12:02, 21:53
time taken 2 h 51 min, 1 h 49 min, 33 min, 4 h 17 min, 2 h 47 min, 2 h 53 min, 10 h 19 min
B 1 10:20   **2** 14:15   **3** 1 h 10 min   **4** 5 min
5 10:30   **6** 12:00   **7** 9:45   **8** 13:30   **9** 12:20
10 10:25   **11** 9:00, 11:15, 14:15   **12** 9:45, 10:30, 12:00, 13:30

Page 54 Calendar
A 1 15.6.08, 25.10.07; 3.5.12, 23.4.11; 25.8.07, 5.2.08; 29.1.02, 20.7.12; 12.3.10, 6.9.09; 20.11.05, 8.12.11
2 6th February 2011, 19th July 2010, 23rd April 2008, 14th August 2012, 7th March 2006, 29th September 2010; 31st January 2012, 30th June 2009, 17th October 2009, 21st May 2007, 24th December 2005, 11th November 2011
B 1 6th April, 14th May, 11th July, 1st March (or 2nd March in a leap year), 30th May, 9th October, 13th January, 8th August   **2** 9th February, 23rd April, 7th September, 7th December; 17th November, 30th May, 22nd January, 11th February
C 1 28, 49;   23, 35;   21, 89;   14, 43
2 31, 24, 74;   52, 65, 17;   22, 8, 28 (or 27 in a leap year)

Page 55 Time, speed and distance
1 40 seconds, 1 minute 20 seconds, 1 minute 40 seconds, 1 minute, 2 minutes, 3 minutes 20 seconds
2 4 km, 8 km, 12 km, 16 km, 2 km, 1 km, 3 km, 6 km, 11 km
3 12 km, 24 km, 36 km, 48 km, 6 km, 3 km, 9 km, 4 km, 8 km, 33 km
4 36 km/h, 24 km/h, 30 km/h, 18 km/h, 9 km/h, 17 km/h, 13 km/h, 26 km/h
5a 40 km/h   **b** 100 km/h   **c** 72 km/h
d 160 km/h   **e** 88 km/h
6 3 h, 2 h 30 min, 1 h 45 min, 2 h 15 min, 1 h 6 min, 54 min, 36 min, 48 min
7 6 h, 4 h 30 min, 1 h 12 min, 48 min, 2 h 24 min, 3 h 30 min, 30 min, 45 min

Page 56 Time, speed and distance
A

Speed (Km/h)	Time (hours)					
	1	$\frac{1}{2}$	$\frac{1}{4}$	$\frac{3}{4}$	$\frac{1}{3}$	$\frac{1}{5}$
30	30 km	15 km	$7\frac{1}{2}$ km	$22\frac{1}{2}$ km	10 km	6 km
60	60 km	30 km	15 km	45 km	20 km	12 km
90	90 km	45 km	$22\frac{1}{2}$ km	$67\frac{1}{2}$ km	30 km	18 km
120	120 km	60 km	30 km	90 km	40 km	24 km
150	150 km	75 km	$37\frac{1}{2}$ km	$112\frac{1}{2}$ km	50 km	30 km

B

Distance (km)	Speed (km/h)					
	10	20	30	40	50	60
10	1 h	30 min	20 min	15 min	12 min	10 min
20	2 h	1 h	40 min	30 min	24 min	20 min
30	3 h	1 h 30 min	1 h	45 min	36 min	30 min
40	4 h	2h	1 h 20 min	1 h	48 min	40 min
50	5 h	2 h 30 min	1 h 40 min	1 h 15 min	1 h	50 min

C

Distance (km)	Time					
	1 h	$\frac{1}{2}$ h	$\frac{1}{4}$ h	$\frac{3}{4}$ h	$\frac{1}{3}$ h	$\frac{1}{5}$ h
12	12 km/h	24 km/h	48 km/h	16 km/h	36 km/h	60 km/h
24	24 km/h	48 km/h	96 km/h	32 km/h	72 km/h	120 km/h
36	36 km/h	72 km/h	144 km/h	48 km/h	108 km/h	180 km/h
48	48 km/h	96 km/h	192 km/h	64 km/h	144 km/h	240 km/h
60	60 km/h	120 km/h	240 km/h	80 km/h	180 km/h	300 km/h

Page 57 Time, speed and distance
A 1 60 km/h, 56 km/h, 52 km/h, 48 km/h, $5\frac{1}{2}$ km/h
2 96 km, 350 km, 495 km, $64\frac{1}{2}$ km, 90 km
3 3 h 30 min, 3 h 5 min, 1 h 45 min, 2 h 12 min, 1 h 6 min
B a 40 km/h **b** 70 km **c** $2\frac{1}{2}$ h
d $292\frac{1}{2}$ km **e** 1 h 20 min **f** 270 km/h

Page 58 Angles
A a 40° **b** 30° **c** 45° **d** 35° **e** 15° **f** 55°
g 125° **h** 150° **i** 145° **j** 115° **k** 105°
l 155°
B 1 and 2 Check the angles your child has drawn.
C 1 and 2 Check the acute and obtuse angles your child has drawn.

Page 59 Bearings and direction
A 1 45° **2** 90° **3** 135° **4** 90° **5** 135°
6 180° **7** 135° **8** 225° **9** 135° **10** 270°
B 310°, 110°, 30°, 250°
C Barton 25°, Endon 50°, Werry 75°, Longton 105°, Smedley 145°, Berry 170°, Nex 190°, Subley 240°, Veal 265°, Perry 295°, Yaln 310°, Dunley 330°
D 1 and **2** Check your child's bearings.

Page 60 Block graphs
A 1 Saturday **2** Tuesday **3** £10 800
4 Saturday **5** £2100 **6** £1800 **7** Thursday, Friday, Saturday **8** £1300 **9** $\frac{3}{4}$
10 Wednesday
B Check your child's graph.
C 1 35, 52, 38, 70, 65, 40 **2** 70 **3** 50
4 35 **5** 2

Page 61 Discontinuous graphs
A 1 Tuesday **2** Monday **3** 275 **4** £275.00
5 55 **6** Friday
B Check your child's graph.
C 1 12th **2** 13th **3** 13th **4** 12th **5** 14th, 15th **6** 6° **7** 14th, 16th **8a** 23° **b** 17°
D Check your child's graph.

Page 62 Straight line and conversion graphs
A 1 10 km **2a** 5 l **b** 15 l **3a** 100 km
b 250 km **c** 170 km **d** 230 km **4** 10 km/l
5a 2·5 l **b** 4·5 l **c** 40 l **d** 35 l
B 1 and 2 Check your child's graphs.
C 1a 75p **b** 90p **c** £1.10 **d** 95p **e** 35p
f 60p **g** 70p **h** £1.05
2a 5 **b** 17 **c** 19 **d** 7 **e** 15 **f** 9
D Check your child's graphs.